Suzann

W9-BYW-531

A Delicate Balance

A PLAY IN THREE ACTS

By Edward Albee

THE PULITZER PRIZE PLAY

1967

SAMUEL FRENCH, INC.

25 WEST 45TH STREET   NEW YORK 10036
7623 SUNSET BOULEVARD   HOLLYWOOD 90046
LONDON   *TORONTO*

FIRST PERFORMANCE

September 12, 1966, New York City, Martin Beck Theatre.

AGNES	*Jessica Tandy*
TOBIAS	*Hume Cronyn*
CLAIRE	*Rosemary Murphy*
EDNA	*Carmen Mathews*
HARRY	*Henderson Forsythe*
JULIA	*Marian Seldes*

Directed by ALAN SCHNEIDER

ACT ONE
Friday night.

ACT TWO

SCENE 1

Early Saturday evening.

SCENE 2

Later that night.

ACT THREE
Early Sunday morning.

THE PLAYERS

AGNES: *A handsome woman in her late 50's.*

TOBIAS: *Her husband, a few years older.*

CLAIRE: *Agnes' sister, several years younger.*

JULIA: *Agnes' and Tobias' daughter, 36, angular.*

EDNA and HARRY: *Very much like Agnes and Tobias.*

THE SCENE

The living room of a large and well-appointed suburban house. Now.

6

A Delicate Balance

ACT ONE

In the library-living room. AGNES *is at library table with
demitasse cup.* TOBIAS *is at chair* D. L., *looking into
cordial bottles.*

AGNES. (*Speaks usually softly, with a tiny hint of a
smile on her face: not sardonic, not sad . . . wistful,
maybe.*) What I find most astonishing—aside from that
belief of mine, (*Crosses* D. L. *to sofa.*) which never ceases
to surprise me by the very fact of its surprising lack of
unpleasantness, the belief that I might very easily—as
they say—lose my mind one day, not that I suspect I
am about to, or am even . . . nearby . . .

TOBIAS. (*He speaks somewhat the same way.*) There
is no saner woman on earth, Agnes. (*Putters at the
bottles.*)

AGNES. . . . for I'm not that sort; merely that it is
not beyond . . . happening: some gentle loosening of the
moorings sending the balloon adrift— (TOBIAS *crosses to
bar.*) and I think that is the only outweighing thing:
adrift; the . . . becoming a stranger in . . . the world,
quite . . . uninvolved, for I never see it as violent, only
a drifting—what are you looking for, Tobias?

TOBIAS. We will all go mad before you. The anisette.
(*He pours drink.*)

AGNES. (*A small happy laugh.*) Thank you, darling.
But I could never do it—go adrift—for what would become of you? Still, what I find most astonishing, aside,
as I said, from that speculation—and I wonder, too,
sometimes, if I am the only one of you to admit to it:
not that *I* may go mad, but that each of you wonders if
each of *you* might not—why on earth do you want
anisette?

7

TOBIAS. (*Considers.*) I thought it might be nice. (*Crosses* D. L.)

AGNES. (*Wrinkles her nose.*) Sticky. I will do cognac, (TOBIAS *crosses to bar.*) It is supposed to be healthy—the speculation, or the assumption, I suppose, that if it occurs to you that you might be, then you are not; but I've never been much comforted by it; it follows, to my mind, that since I speculate I might, some day, (TOBIAS *opens new cognac bottle.*) or early evening I think more likely—some autumn dusk—go quite mad, then I very well might. (*Bright laugh.*) Some autumn dusk: Tobias at his desk, looks up from all those awful bills, and sees his Agnes, mad as a hatter, chewing the ribbons on her dress. . . . (*Crosses to* L. *chair.*)

TOBIAS. (*Pouring.*) Cognac?

AGNES. Yes; Agnes Sit-by-the-fire, her mouth full of ribbons, her mind aloft, adrift; nothing to do with the poor old thing but put her in a bin somewhere, sell the house, move to Tucson, say, and pine in the good sun, and live to be a hundred and four. (*He gives her her cognac.*) Thank you, darling.

TOBIAS. Cognac is sticky, too. (*Kisses her forehead.*)

AGNES. Yes, but it's nicer. (TOBIAS *starts* L.) Sit by me, hm?

TOBIAS. (*Puts cushion on floor near her and sits on it. Raises his glass.*) To my mad lady, ribbons dangling.

AGNES. (*Smiles.*) And, of course, I haven't worn the ribbon dress since Julia's remarriage. Second? No, first. Tom. Not Charlie. Are you comfortable?

TOBIAS. For a little.

AGNES. What astonishes me most—aside from my theoretically healthy fear—no, not fear, how silly of me—healthy speculation that I might some day become an embarrassment to you . . . what I find most astonishing in this world, and with all my years . . . is Claire.

TOBIAS. (*Curious.*) Claire? Why?

AGNES. That anyone—be they one's sister, or not—can

be so . . . well, I don't want to use an unkind word,
'cause we're cozy here, aren't we?

TOBIAS. (*Smiled warning.*) Maybe.

AGNES. As the saying has it, the one thing sharper than
a serpent's tooth is a sister's ingratitude.

TOBIAS. (*Getting up, putting cushion on ottoman.*)
The saying does not have it that way.

AGNES. Should. Why are you moving?

TOBIAS. It's getting uncomfortable.

AGNES. (*Semi-serious razzing.*) Things get hot, move
off, huh? Yes?

TOBIAS. (*Not rising to it, crossing to* D. L. *chair.*) I'm
not as young as either of us once was.

AGNES. (*Toasting him.*) I'm as young as the day I
married you—though I'm certain I don't look it—because
you're a very good husband . . . most of the time. But
I was talking about Claire, or was beginning to.

TOBIAS. (*Knowing shaking of the head.*) Yes, you were.

AGNES. If I were to list the mountain of my burdens—
if I had a thick pad and a month to spare—that bending
my shoulders *most,* with the possible exception of Julia's
trouble with marriage, would be your—it must be in-
stinctive, I think, or *reflex,* that's more like it—your
reflex defense of everything that Claire . . .

TOBIAS. (*Very nice, but there is steel underneath.*)
Stop it, Agnes.

AGNES. (*A little laugh.*) Are you going to throw something at me? Your glass? My goodness, I hope not . . .
that awful anisette all over everything.

TOBIAS. (*Patient; puts glass on* D. L. *table.*) No.

AGNES. (*Quietly daring him.*) What then?

TOBIAS. (*Looking at his hand.*) I shall sit very
quietly . . .

TOBIAS. . . . yes, and I shall will you to apologize to
your sister for what I must in truth tell you I thought a
most . . .

AGNES. Apologize! To her? To Claire? I have spent

my adult life apologizing *for* her; (*Crosses to* R. *of sofa.*) I will not double my humiliation by apologizing *to* her.

TOBIAS. (*Mocking an epigram.*) One does not apologize to those for whom one must?

AGNES. (*Winking slowly.*) Neat.

TOBIAS. Succinct, but one of the rules of an aphorism . . .

AGNES. An epigram, I thought.

TOBIAS. (*Small smile.*) An epigram is usually satiric, and you . . .

AGNES. . . . and I am grimly serious. Yes?

TOBIAS. I fear so.

AGNES. (*Crosses to Upstage of* L. *chair.*) To revert specifically from Claire to . . . her effect, what *would* you do were I to . . . spill my marbles?

TOBIAS. (*Shrugs.*) Put you in a bin somewhere, sell the house and move to Tucson. Pine in the hot sun and live forever.

AGNES. (*Ponders it.*) Hmmm, I bet you would.

TOBIAS. (*Friendly.*) Hurry, though.

AGNES. Oh, I'll *try.* (*Crosses to* R.) It won't be simple paranoia, though, (TOBIAS *takes cigar from humidor.*) I know that. I've tried so hard, to . . . well, you know how little I vary; goodness, (*At sofa* R.) I can't even raise my voice except in the most calamitous of events, and I find that both joy and sorrow work their . . . wonders on me more . . . evenly, slowly, within, than most: a suntan rather than a scalding. There are no mountains in my life . . . nor chasms. It is a rolling, pleasant land . . . verdant, my darling, thank you.

TOBIAS. (*Cutting a cigar.*) We do what we can.

AGNES. (*Little laugh.*) Our motto. If we should ever go downhill, have a crest made, join things, we must have that put in Latin— We do what we can— (TOBIAS *crosses to table* L. *of sofa.*) on your blazers, over the mantel; maybe we could do it in the linen, as well. . . .

TOBIAS. (*Gets matches from table.*) Do you think I should go to Claire's room?

AGNES. (*Silence: then stony, firm.*) No. (TOBIAS *shrugs, lights his cigar.*) Either she will be down, or not.

TOBIAS. We do what we can?

AGNES. Of course. (*Silence.* TOBIAS *crosses* R., *lights cigar.*) So, it will not be simple paranoia. Schizophrenia, on the other hand, is far more likely—even given the unlikelihood. I believe it can be chemically induced . . . (*Smiles.* TOBIAS *crosses to* R. *chair.*) if all else should fail; if sanity, such as it is, should become too much. There are times when I think it would be so . . . proper, if one could take a pill—or even inject—just . . . remove.

TOBIAS. (*Fairly dry.*) You should take drugs, my dear.

AGNES. Ah, but those are temporary; even addiction is a repeated temporary . . . stilling. I am concerned with peace . . . not mere relief. And I am not a compulsive—like . . . like some . . . like our dear Claire, say.

TOBIAS. Be kind. Please?

AGNES. I think I should want to have it fully . . . even on the chance I could not . . . come back. Wouldn't that be terrible, though? To have done it, induced, if naturally looked unlikely and the hope was there? (*Wonder in her voice.*) Not be able to come back? Why did you put my cognac in the tiny glass?

TOBIAS. (*Rising, going to her.*) Oh . . . I'm sorry. . . .

AGNES. (*Holding her glass out to him; he takes it from her.*) I'm not a sipper tonight; I'm a breather: my nose buried in the glass, all the wonder there, and very silent.

TOBIAS. (*At bar getting her a new cognac.*) I thought Claire was much better tonight. I didn't see any need for you to give her such a going-over.

AGNES. (*Weary.*) Claire was *not* better tonight. Honestly, Tobias!

TOBIAS. (*Clinging to his conviction.*) I thought she was.

AGNES. (*Putting an end to it.*) Well, she was *not*.

TOBIAS. (*Crosses to* AGNES *with snifter glass of brandy.*) Still . . .

AGNES. (*Taking her new drink.*) Thank you. I have

decided, all things considered, (*Takes* TOBIAS' *hand and pulls him down to sofa.*) that I shall not induce, that's all the years we have put up with each other's wiles and crotchets have earned us each other's company. And I promise you as well that I shall think good thoughts—healthy ones, positive—to ward off madness, should it come by . . . uninvited.

TOBIAS. (*Smiles.*) You mean I have no hope of Tucson?

AGNES. None.

TOBIAS. (*Mock sadness.*) Hélas . . .

AGNES. You have hope, only, of growing even older than you are in the company of your steady wife, your alcoholic sister-in-law and occasional visits . . . from our melancholy Julia. (*A little sad.*) That is what you have, my dear Tobias. Will it do?

TOBIAS. (*A little sad, too, but warmth.*) It will do.

AGNES. (*Happy.*) I've never doubted that it would. (*Hears something, says sourly.*) Hark. (CLAIRE *has entered* U. C.) Did I hear someone?

TOBIAS. (*Sees* CLAIRE *standing, uncomfortably, away from them.*) Ah, there you are. I said to Agnes just a moment ago . . .

CLAIRE. (*To* AGNES' *back, a rehearsed speech, gone through but hated.*) I must apologize, Agnes; I'm . . . very sorry.

AGNES. (*Not looking at her; mock surprise.*) But what are you sorry *for*, Claire?

CLAIRE. (*Crossing to* R. *of sofa.*) I apologize that my nature is such to bring out in you the full force of your brutality.

TOBIAS. (*To placate, crossing to* L. *of sofa.*) Look, now, I think we can do without any of this sort of . . .

AGNES. (*Rises from her chair, proceeds toward exiting.*) *If* you come to the dinner table unsteady, *if* when you try to say good evening and weren't the autumn colors lovely today you are nothing but vowels, and *if* one smells the vodka on you from across the room—and *don't* tell me again, *either* of you! that vodka leaves nothing on the breath: (CLAIRE *crosses to* R. *chair.*) if you are expecting it, if you are sadly and wearily expecting it, it *does—if* these conditions exist . . . *persist* . . . then the reaction of one who is burdened by her love is not brutality—though it would be excused, believe me!—not brutality at all, but the souring side of love. If I scold, it is because I wish I needn't. If I am sharp, it is because I am neither less nor more than human, and if I am to be accused once again of making too much of things, let me remind you that it is my manner and not the matter. I apologize for being articulate. Tobias, I'm going to call Julia, I think. Is it one or two hours difference? . . . I can never recall.

TOBIAS. (*Dry.*) Three.

AGNES. Ah, yes. Well, be kind to Claire, dear. She is . . . injured. (*Exits. A brief silence.*)

CLAIRE. Be kind to Claire, dear. She is . . . injured.

TOBIAS. Ah, well.

CLAIRE. (*Crosses* D. L. *to sofa.*) I have never known whether to applaud or cry. Or, rather, I never know which would be the more appreciated—expected.

TOBIAS. (*Rather sadly.*) You are a great damn fool.

CLAIRE. (*Sadly.*) Yes. Why is she calling Julia?

TOBIAS. Do you want a quick brandy before she comes back?

CLAIRE. (*Laughs some.*) Not at all; a public one. (TOBIAS *crosses to bar, pours brandy in snifter.*) Fill the balloon half up, and I shall sip it ladylike, and when she . . . glides back in, I shall lie on the floor and balance the glass on my forehead. That will give her occasion for another paragraph, (TOBIAS *crosses* R. *to* CLAIRE *with brandy.*) and your ineffectual stop-it-now's.

TOBIAS. You *are* a great damn fool.

CLAIRE. Is Julia having another divorce?

TOBIAS. Hell, I don't know.

CLAIRE. (*Takes the glass.* TOBIAS *crosses* U. R. *to sofa.*) It's only your daughter. Thank you. I should imagine—

from all that I have . . . watched, that it is come-home time. (*Offhand.*) Why don't you kill Agnes?

TOBIAS. (*Very offhand.*) Oh, no, I couldn't do that.

CLAIRE. Better still, why don't you wait till Julia separates and comes back here, all sullen and confused, and take a gun and blow all our heads off? . . . Agnes first—through respect, of course, then poor Julia, and finally—if you have the kindness for it—me?

TOBIAS. (*Kind, triste.*) Do you really want me to shoot you?

CLAIRE. I want you to shoot Agnes first. Then I'll think about it.

TOBIAS. But it would have to be an act of passion—out of my head, and all that. I doubt I'd stand around with the gun smoking, Julia locked in her room screaming, wait for you to decide if you wanted it or not.

CLAIRE. But unless you kill Agnes . . . how shall I ever know whether I want to live? (*Incredulous.*) An act of passion!?

TOBIAS. (*Rather hurt.*) Well . . . yes.

CLAIRE. (*Laughs.*) Oh, my; *that's* funny.

TOBIAS. (*Same.*) I'm sorry.

CLAIRE. (*Friendly laugh.*) Oh, my darling Tobias, *I'm* sorry, but I just don't see you in the role, that's all— outraged, maddened into action, proceeding by reflex . . . Can you see yourself, though? In front of the judge? Predictable, stolid Tobias? (TOBIAS *crosses* U. L. *of sofa.*) "It all went blank, your honor. One moment, there I was, deep in my chair, drinking my . . ." What is that?

TOBIAS. Anisette.

CLAIRE. "Anisette." Really? Anisette?

TOBIAS. (*Slightly edgy.*) I *like* it. (*At* L. *chair.*)

CLAIRE. (*Wrinkles her nose.*) Sticky. "There I was, your honor, one moment in my chair, sipping at my anisette . . . and the next thing I knew . . . they were all lying about, different rooms, heads blown off, the gun still in my hand. I . . . I have no recollection of it, sir."

Can you imagine that, Tobias? (*She lies on sofa, her head to* R.)

TOBIAS. Of course, with all of you dead, your brains lying around in the rugs, there'd be no one to say it *wasn't* an act of passion.

CLAIRE. Leave me till last. A breeze might rise and stir the ashes. . . .

TOBIAS. Who's that?

CLAIRE. No one, I think. Just sounds like it should be.

TOBIAS. Why don't you go back to your . . . thing . . . to your alcoholics thing?

CLAIRE. (*Half serious.*) Because I don't like the people. . . .

TOBIAS. What is it called?

CLAIRE. Anonymous.

TOBIAS. Yes; that. Why don't you go back?

CLAIRE. (*Suddenly rather ugly. Crosses to* R. *coffee table, kneels.*) Why don't you mind your own hooting business?

TOBIAS. (*Offended.*) I'm sorry, Claire.

CLAIRE. (*Kisses at him.*) Because.

TOBIAS. It was better.

CLAIRE. (*Holds her glass out; he hesitates.*) Be a good brother-in-law; it's only the first I'm not supposed to have.

TOBIAS. (*Takes glass, crosses* L. *to bar.*) *I* thought it was better.

CLAIRE. Thank you. (*Lies on the floor.*) You mean Agnes thought it was better.

TOBIAS. (*Kindly, calmly.*) No, I thought so too. That it would be.

CLAIRE. I told you: not our type; nothing in common with them. When you used to go to business—before you became a squire, parading around in jodhpurs, confusing the gardener . . .

TOBIAS. (*Crossing to* CLAIRE *with brandy. Hurt.*) I've never done any such thing.

CLAIRE. Before all that . . . (TOBIAS *crosses to bar.*

She smiles, chuckles.) sweet Tobias . . . when you used to spend all your time in town . . . with your business friends, your indistinguishable if not necessarily similar friends . . . what did you have in common with them?

TOBIAS. Well, uh . . . well, everything. (*Maybe slightly on the defensive, but more . . . vague.*) Our business; we all mixed well, were friends away from the office, too . . . clubs, our . . . an, an environment, I guess.

CLAIRE. Unh-huh. But what did you have in common with them? Even Harry: your very best friend . . . in all the world—as far as you know; I mean, you haven't met everybody . . . (*Sits up.*) are you switching from anisette?

TOBIAS. (*Pouring himself brandy.*) Doesn't go for a long time. All right?

CLAIRE. Doesn't matter to *me*. Your very best friend . . . Tell me, dear Tobias; what do you have in common with him? Hm?

TOBIAS. (*Softly, steps in to* R.) Please, Claire . . .

CLAIRE. What do you really have in common with your very best friend . . . (TOBIAS *crosses up to platform.*) 'cept the coincidence of having cheated on your wives in the same summer with the same woman . . . girl . . . woman? What except that? And hardly a distinction. I believe she was upended that whole July.

TOBIAS. (*Rather tight-mouthed.*) If you'll forgive me, Claire, common practice is hardly coincidence. (*Crosses* U. R. *on platform.*)

CLAIRE. Poor girl, poor whatever-she-was that hot and very *wet* July. (*Hard.*) The distinction would have been to have not: to have been the one or two of the very, very many and oh, God, similar who did not upend the poor . . . unfamiliar thing that dry and oh, so wet July.

TOBIAS. Please! Agnes!

CLAIRE. (*Quieter.*) Of course, you had the wanton only once, while Harry! Good friend Harry, I have it from the horse's mouth, was on top for good and keeps twice,

(TOBIAS *crosses Down to* R. *chair.*) with a third try not
so hot in the gardener's shed, with the mulch, or whatever it is, and the orange pots. . . .

TOBIAS. (*Quietly.*) Shut your mouth.

CLAIRE. (*Crosses on knees, kisses* TOBIAS *on forehead.*)
All right. (*Down again.* R. *of coffee table.*) What was her
name?

TOBIAS. (*A little sad.*) I don't remember.

CLAIRE. (*Shrugs.*) No matter; she's gone. (*Brighter.*)
Would you give friend Harry the shirt off your back, as
they say?

TOBIAS. (*Relieved to be on something else.*) I *suppose*
I would. He *is* my best friend.

CLAIRE. (*Nicely.*) How sad does that make you?

TOBIAS. (*Looks at her for a moment, then:*) Not much;
some; not much.

CLAIRE. No one to listen to Bruckner with you; no one
to tell you're sick of golf; no one to admit to that—now
and then—you're suddenly frightened and you don't know
why?

TOBIAS. (*Mild surprise.*) Frightened? No.

CLAIRE. (*Pause; smile.*) All right. Would you like to
know what happened last time I climbed the stairs to
the fancy alkie club, and why I've not gone back? What
I have *not* in common with those people?

TOBIAS. (*Not too enthusiastic.*) Sure.

CLAIRE. (*Chuckles.*) Poor Tobias. "Sure." Light me a
cigarette? (TOBIAS *hesitates a moment, crosses to table*
L. *of sofa. Lights cigarette then crosses to her.*) That will
give me everything. (*He hands the lighted cigarette to
her; she is still on the floor.*) I need. A smoke, a sip and
a good hard surface. Thank you. (*Laughs a bit at that.*)

TOBIAS. (*Standing over her.*) Comfy?

CLAIRE. (*Raises her two arms, one with the cigarette,
the other the brandy glass; it is a casual invitation.*
TOBIAS *looks at her for a moment, moves a little away.
Crosses to* L. *chair.*) Very. Do you remember the spring
I moved out, the time I was *really* sick with the stuff:

was drinking like the famous fish? Was a source of great embarrassment? So that you and Agnes set me up in the apartment near the station, and Agnes was *so* good about coming to see me? (TOBIAS *sighs heavily.*) Sorry.

TOBIAS. (*Pleading a little.*) When will it all . . . just go in the past . . . forget itself?

CLAIRE. When all the defeats are done, admitted. When memory takes over and corrects fact . . . makes it tolerable. When Agnes lies on her deathbed.

TOBIAS. Do you know that Agnes has . . . such wonderful control I haven't seen her cry in . . . for the longest time . . . no matter what?

CLAIRE. Warn me when she's coming; I'll act drunk. Pretend you're very sick, Tobias, like you were with the stomach business, but pretend you feel your insides are all green, and stink, and mixed up, and your eyes hurt and you're half deaf and your brain keeps turning off, and you've got peripheral neuritis and you can hardly walk and you hate. You hate with the same green stinking sickness you feel your bowels have turned into . . . yourself, and *everybody*. Hate, and, oh, God!! you want love, l-o-v-e, so badly—comfort and snuggling is what you really mean, of course—but you hate, and you notice—with a sort of detachment that amuses you, you think—that you're more like an animal every day . . . you snarl, and *grab* for things, and hide things and forget where you hid them like not-very-bright dogs, and you wash less, prefer to *be* washed, and once or twice you've actually soiled your bed and laid in it because you can't get up . . . pretend all that. No, you don't like that, Tobias?

TOBIAS. I don't know why you want to . . .

CLAIRE. You want to know what it's like to be an alkie, don't you, boy?

TOBIAS. (*Sad.*) Sure.

CLAIRE. (*A step* U. R. *of sofa.*) Pretend all that. So the guy you're spending your bottles with starts you going to the old A.A. And, you sit there at the alkie club and watch the . . . better ones—not recovered, for once an alkie, always, and you'd better remember it, or you're gone the first time you pass a saloon—you watch the better ones get up and tell their stories.

TOBIAS. (*Wistful, triste.*) Once you drop . . . you can come back up part way . . . but never . . . really back again. Always . . . descent.

CLAIRE. (*Gently, to a child.*) Well, that's life, baby.

TOBIAS. You are a great, damn fool.

CLAIRE. (*Crosses* U. L.) But, I'm not an alcoholic. I am not now and never was.

TOBIAS. (*Shaking his head.*) All the promise . . . all the chance . . .

CLAIRE. It would be so much simpler if I *were*. An alcoholic. (*She will rise and re-enact during this.*) So, one night, one month, sometime, I'd had one martini—as a Test to see if I could—which, given my . . . stunning self-discipline, had become three, and I felt . . . rather daring and nicely detached and a little bigger than life and not snarling yet. (*Crosses* U. C. *to arch.*) So I marched, more or less straight, straight up to the front of the room, hall, and faced my peers. And I looked them over—all of them, trying so hard, grit and guilt and failing and trying again and loss . . . and I had a moment's—sweeping—pity and disgust, and I almost cried, but I didn't—like sister like sister, by God—and I heard myself say, in my little-girl voice—and there were a lot of different me's by then— "I am a alcoholic." (*Little-girl voice.*) "My name is Claire, and I am a alcoholic." (*Directly to* TOBIAS.) You try it.

TOBIAS. (*Rather vague, but not babytalk.*) My name is . . . My name is Claire, and I am an alcoholic.

CLAIRE. A alcoholic.

TOBIAS. (*Vaguer.*) A alcoholic.

CLAIRE. "My name is Claire, and I am a . . . alcoholic." (*Crosses* R. *of sofa.*) Now, I was supposed to go on, *you* know, say how bad I was, and didn't want to be, and How It Happened, and What I Wanted To Happen, and Would They Help Me Help Myself . . . but I just stood there for a . . . ten seconds maybe, and then I curtsied; I made my little-girl curtsy, and on my little-girl feet I padded back to my chair. (*Crosses to* L. *chair.*)

TOBIAS. (*After a pause; embarrassedly.*) Did they laugh at you?

CLAIRE. Well, an agnostic in the holy of holies doesn't get much camaraderie, a little patronizing, maybe. Oh, they were taken by the *vaude*ville, don't misunderstand me. But the one lady was nice. ᴐhe came up to me later and said, "You've taken the first step, dear."

TOBIAS. (*Hopeful.*) That was nice of her.

CLAIRE. (*Amused.*) She didn't say the first step toward *what*, of course. Sanity, *in*sanity, revelation, self-deception. . . .

TOBIAS. (*Not much help.*) Change . . . sometimes . . . no matter what . . .

CLAIRE. (*Cheerful laugh.*) Count on you, Tobias . . . snappy phrase every time. (*Crosses to coffee table.*) But it *hooked* me—the applause, the stage presence . . . that beginning; no school tot had more gold stars for never missing class. I went; oh, God, I *did*.

TOBIAS. But stopped.

CLAIRE. Until I learned . . . (*She crosses to bar; refills her glass; then crosses to* R. *of coffee table and squats on floor.* AGNES *enters, unobserved by either* TOBIAS *or* CLAIRE.) . . . and being a slow student in my young middle-age, slowly . . . that I was not nor had ever been . . . a alcoholic . . . or an. Either. What I did not have in common with those people. That they were alcoholics, and I was not. That I was just a drunk. That they couldn't help it; I could, and wouldn't. That they were sick, and I was merely . . . willful.

AGNES. I have talked to Julia. (*Steps to* U. R.)

TOBIAS. Ah! How is she?

AGNES. (*Walking by* CLAIRE.) My, what an odd glass to put a soft drink in. Tobias, you have a quiet sense of humor, after all.

TOBIAS. Now, Agnes . . .

CLAIRE. He has not!

AGNES. (*Rather heavy-handed.*) Well, it *can't* be brandy; Tobias is a grown-up, and knows far better than to . . .

CLAIRE. (*Harsh, waving her glass.*) A toast to you, sweet sister; I drink your—not health; persistence—in good, hard brandy, *âge inconnu.*

AGNES. (*Quiet, tight smile, ignoring* CLAIRE; *steps to* TOBIAS.) It *would* serve you right, my dear Tobias, were I to go away, drift off. You would not have a woman left about you—only Claire and Julia . . . not even people; it would serve you right.

CLAIRE. (*Great mocking.*) But I'm not an alcoholic, baby!

TOBIAS. She . . . she can drink . . . a little.

AGNES. (*There is true passion here; we see under the calm a little.*) I WILL NOT TOLERATE IT!! I WILL NOT HAVE YOU! (*Softer, but tight-lipped.*) Oh, God. I wouldn't mind for a moment if you filled your bathtub with it, lowered yourself in it, DROWNED! I rather wish you would. It would give me the peace of mind to know you could do something well, thoroughly. If you want to kill (*Crosses to* R. *chair.*) yourself—then do it *right!*

TOBIAS. Please, Agnes . . . (*Crosses to* R. *of sofa.*)

AGNES. What I cannot stand is the selfishness! Those of you who want to die . . . and take your whole lives doing it.

CLAIRE. (*Lazy, but with loathing under it, crossing* D. R. *of* R. *chair.*) Your wife is a perfectionist; they are *very* difficult to live with, these people.

TOBIAS. (*To* AGNES, *a little pleading in it.*) She isn't an alcoholic . . . she says; she can drink some.

CLAIRE. (*Little-child statement, but not babytalk.*) I am not a alcoholic!

AGNES. We think that's very nice. We shall all rest easier to know that it is willful; that the vomit and the tears, the muddy mind, (TOBIAS *crosses to* L. *sofa.*) the falls and the absences, the cigarettes out on the table-tops, the calls from the club to come and get you please . . . that they are all . . . willful, that it *can* be helped. (*Scathing, but softly.*) If you are not an alcoholic, you are beyond forgiveness.

CLAIRE. (*Ibid.*) Well, I've been that for a long time, haven't I, sweetheart?

AGNES. (*Not looking at either of them.*) If we change for the worse with drink, we are an alcoholic. It is as simple as that.

CLAIRE. And who is to say!

AGNES. I!

CLAIRE. (*A litany.*) If we are to live here, on Tobias' charity, then we are subject to the will of his wife. If we were asked, at our father's dying . . .

AGNES. (*Final.*) Those are the ground rules.

(TOBIAS *sits on sofa.*)

CLAIRE. (*A sad smile.*) Tobias? (*Pause.*) Nothing? (*Pause; crosses to* R. *arm of sofa. Leans in.*) Are those the ground rules? Nothing? Too . . . settled? Too . . . dried up? Gone? (*Nicely.*) All right. (*Back to* AGNES, *crossing* R.) Very well, then, Agnes, you win. I shall be an alcoholic. (*The smile too sweet.*) What are you going to do about it?

AGNES. (*Regards* CLAIRE *for a moment, then decides she*—CLAIRE—*is not in the room with them.* AGNES *will ignore* CLAIRE'S *coming comments until otherwise indicated.* TOBIAS *will do this, too, but uncomfortably, embarrassedly.*) Tobias, you will be unhappy to know it, I suppose, or of mixed emotions, certainly, but Julia is coming home

CLAIRE. (*A brief laugh.*) Naturally. (*Up to* R. *chair.*)

TOBIAS. Yes?

AGNES. She is leaving Douglas, which is no surprise to *me*.

TOBIAS. But, wasn't Julia happy? You didn't tell me anything about . . .

AGNES. If Julia were happy, she would not be coming home. *I* don't want her here, God knows. I mean she's welcome, of course . . .

CLAIRE. Right on schedule, once every three years. . . .

AGNES. (*Closes her eyes for a moment, to keep ignoring* CLAIRE.) . . . It *is* her home, we are her parents, the *two* of us, and we have our obligations to her, and I have reached an age, Tobias, when I wish we were always alone, you and I, without . . . hangers-on . . . or anyone.

CLAIRE. (*Cheerful but firm.*) Well, I'm not going.

AGNES. (*Crosses to sofa.*) . . . but if she and Doug are through—and I'm not suggesting *she* is in the right—then her place is properly here, as for some it is not.

CLAIRE. One, two, three, four, down they go.

TOBIAS. Well, I'd like to talk to Doug.

AGNES. (*As if the opposite answer were expected from her.*) I wish you would! If you had talked to Tom, or Charlie, yes! even Charlie, or . . . uh . . .

CLAIRE. Phil?

AGNES. (*No recognition of* CLAIRE *helping her.*) . . . Phil, it might have done some good. If you've decided to assert yourself, finally, too late, I imagine . . .

CLAIRE. Damned if you do, damned if you don't.

AGNES. . . . Julia might, at the very least, come to think her father cares, and that might be consolation—if not help.

TOBIAS. I'll . . . I'll talk to Doug.

CLAIRE. Why don't you invite him *here?* And while you're at it, bring the others along.

AGNES. (*Some reproach.*) And you might talk to Julia, too. You don't, very much.

TOBIAS. Yes.

CLAIRE. (*A mocking sing-song.*)
> Philip loved to gamble.
> Charlie loved the boys,

Tom went after women,
Douglas . . .

AGNES. (*Turning on* CLAIRE.) *Will* you stop that? (*Crosses* U. R. *of sofa*.)

CLAIRE. Ooh, I *am* here, after all. I exist!

AGNES. Why don't you go off on a vacation, Claire, now that Julia's coming home again? Why don't you go to Kentucky, or Tennessee, and visit the distilleries? Or why don't you lock yourself in your room, or find yourself a bar with an apartment in the back . . . (*Crosses* U. L. *to sofa*.)

CLAIRE. Or! Agnes; why don't you die?

(AGNES *and* CLAIRE *lock eyes, stay still*.)

TOBIAS. (*Not rising from sofa, talks more or less to himself*.) If I saw some point to it, I might—if I saw some reason, chance. If I thought I might . . . break through to her, and say, "Julia . . . ," but then what would I say? "Julia . . ." Then, nothing.

AGNES. (*Breaking eye contact with* CLAIRE, *crossing* L.; *says, not looking at either*.) If we do not love someone . . . never have loved them . . .

TOBIAS. (*Soft correction*.) No; there can be silence, even having.

AGNES. (*More curious than anything*.) Do you really want me dead, Claire?

CLAIRE. Wish, yes. Want? I don't know; probably. though I might regret it if I had it.

AGNES. Remember the serpent's tooth, Tobias.

TOBIAS. (*Recollection*.) The cat that I had.

AGNES. Hm?

TOBIAS. The cat that I had . . . when I was—well, a year or so before I *met* you. She was very old; I'd had her since I was a kid; she must have been fifteen, or more. An alley cat. She didn't like people very much, I think; when (AGNES *crosses to* L. *chair*.) people came . . . she'd . . . pick up and walk away. She liked *me;* or, rather, when I was alone with her I could see she was content;

she'd sit on my lap. I don't know if she was happy, but she was content.

AGNES. Yes.

TOBIAS. And how the thing happened I don't really know. She . . . one day she . . . well, one day I realized she no longer liked me. No, that's not right; one day I realized she must have stopped liking me some time before. One evening I was alone, home, and I was suddenly aware of her absence, not just that she wasn't in the room with *me*, but that she hadn't been, in rooms with me, watching me shave . . . just *about* . . . for . . . I couldn't place *how* long. She hadn't gone *away*, you understand; well, she *had*, but she hadn't run off. I knew she was *around;* I remembered I had caught sight of her—from time to time—under a chair, moving out of a room, but it was only when I realized something had happened that I could give any pattern to things that had . . . that I'd noticed. She didn't like me any more. It was that simple.

CLAIRE. Well, she was old.

TOBIAS. No, it wasn't that. She didn't like me any more. I tried to force myself on her.

AGNES. Whatever do you mean?

TOBIAS. I'd close her in a room with me; I'd pick her up, and I'd *make* her sit in my lap; I'd make her stay there when she didn't want to. But it didn't work; she'd abide it, but she'd get down when she could, go away.

CLAIRE. Maybe she was ill.

TOBIAS. No, she wasn't; I had her to the vet. She didn't like me any more. One night—I was *fixed* on it now—I had her in the room with me, and on my lap for the . . . the what, the fifth time the same evening, and she lay there, with her back to me, and she wouldn't purr, and I *knew:* I knew she was just waiting till she could get down, and I said, "Damn you, you like me; God damn it, you stop this! I haven't *done* anything to you." And I shook her; I had my hands around her shoulders, and I shook her . . . and she bit me; hard;

and she hissed at me. And so I hit her. With my open hand, I hit her, smack, right across the head. I . . . I *hated* her!

AGNES. Did you hurt her badly?

TOBIAS. Yes; well, not badly; she . . . I must have hurt her ear some; she shook her head a lot for a day or so. And . . . you see, there was no *reason*. She and I had lived together and been, well, you know, friends, and . . . there was no *reason*. And I hated her for that. I hated her, well, I suppose because I was being accused of something, of . . . failing. But, I hadn't been cruel, by design; if I'd been neglectful, well, my life was . . . I resented it. I resented having a . . . being judged. Being *betrayed*.

CLAIRE. What did you do?

TOBIAS. I had *lived* with her; I had done . . . *everything*. And . . . and if there was a, any responsibility I'd failed in . . . well . . . there was nothing I could *do*. And, and I was being accused.

CLAIRE. Yes; what did you do?

TOBIAS. (*Defiance and self-loathing.*) I had her killed.

AGNES. (*Kindly correcting.*) You had her put to sleep. She was old. You had her put to sleep.

TOBIAS. (*Correcting.*) I had her killed. I took her to the vet and he took her . . . he took her into the back and (*Louder.*) he gave her an injection and killed her! I had her *killed!*

AGNES. (*After a pause.*) Well, what else could you have done? There was nothing to be done; there was no . . . meeting between you.

TOBIAS. I might have tried longer. I might have gone on, as long as cats live, the same way. I might have worn a hair shirt, locked myself in the house with her, done penance. For *something*. For *what*. God knows.

CLAIRE. You probably did the right *thing*. Distasteful alternatives; the less . . . ugly choice.

TOBIAS. Was it? (*A silence from them* ALL.)

AGNES. (*Noticing the window.*) Was that a car in the drive?

TOBIAS. "If we do not love someone . . . never have loved someone . . ."

CLAIRE. (*An abrupt, brief laugh, crosses U. L. of sofa.*) Oh, stop it! "Love" is not the problem. You love Agnes and Agnes loves Julia and Julia loves me and I love you. We all love each other; yes we do. We love each other.

TOBIAS. Yes?

CLAIRE. (*Something of a sneer.*) Yes; to the depths of our self-pity and our greed. What else but love?

TOBIAS. (*Crosses to bar.*) Error?

CLAIRE. (*Laughs.*) Quite possibly: love and error.

(*There is a KNOCK at the door; AGNES answers it. CLAIRE crosses to D. L. chair.*)

AGNES. Edna? Harry? What a surprise! Tobias, it's Harry and Edna. Come in. Why don't you take off your . . .

(*HARRY and EDNA enter. They seem somewhat ill at ease, strained for such close friends.*)

TOBIAS. (*Crosses U. C. to arch.*) Edna!

EDNA. Hello, Tobias.

HARRY. (*Rubbing his hands; attempt at being bluff.*) Well, now!

TOBIAS. Harry!

HARRY. Tobias.

CLAIRE. (*Too much surprise.*) Edna! (*Imitates HARRY's gruff voice.*) Hello, there, Harry!

EDNA. Hello, dear Claire! (*A little timid.*) Hello, Agnes.

HARRY. (*Somewhat distant.*) Evening . . . Claire.

TOBIAS. How are you, Edna? (*He stays at C. arch.*)

AGNES. (*Jumping in, just as a tiny silence commences. Crosses to R. chair and sits.*) Sit **down**. We were just having a cordial. . . . (*Curiously loud.*) Have you been . . . out? Uh, to the club?

(EDNA *crosses* D. R. *to sofa.*)

HARRY. (*Is he ignoring* AGNES' *question? Crosses* U. L. *of sofa.*) I like this room.

AGNES. To the club?

CLAIRE. (*Exaggerated, but not unkind.*) How's the old Harry?

HARRY. (*Self-pity entering. A step* D. L.) Pretty well, Claire, not as good as I'd like, but . . .

EDNA. Harry's been having his shortness of breath again.

HARRY. (*Generally.*) I can't breathe sometimes . . . for just a bit.

TOBIAS. (*Joining them* ALL. *Crosses* U. L. *of sofa.*) Well, two sets of tennis, you know.

EDNA. (*As if she can't remember something.*) What have you done to the room, Agnes?

AGNES. (*Looks around with a little apprehension, then relief.*) Oh, the summer *things* are off.

EDNA. Of course.

AGNES. (*Persisting in it, a strained smile.*) Have you been to the club?

HARRY. (*To* TOBIAS.) I was talking to Edna, 'bout having our books done in leather; bound. (*Crosses to* R. *sofa.*)

TOBIAS. (*Crosses to* L. *chair.*) Oh? Yes? (*Brief silence.*)

CLAIRE. The question—'less I'm going deaf from all the alcohol—was (*Southern accent.*) "Have you-all been to the club?"

AGNES. (*Nervous, apologetic covering.*) I wondered!

HARRY. (*Hesistant.*) Why . . . no, no.

EDNA. (*Ibid.*) Why, why, no, Agnes. . . .

AGNES. I wondered, for I thought perhaps you'd dropped by here on your way from there.

HARRY. . . . no, no . . .

AGNES. . . . or perhaps that we were having a party, and I'd lost a day. . . .

HARRY. No, we were . . . just sitting home.

EDNA. (*Some condolence.*) Agnes.

HARRY. (*Looking at his hands.*) Just . . . sitting home.

AGNES. (*Cheerful, but lack of anything better to say.*) Well.

TOBIAS. (*Crosses to L. chair.*) Glad you're here! Party or not!

HARRY. (*Relieved.*) Good to see you, Tobias!

EDNA. (*All smiles.*) How is Julia?

CLAIRE. (*Crosses U. L.*) Wrong question. May I have some brandy, Tobias? (*She hands* TOBIAS *her glass and crosses to sofa.* TOBIAS *crosses to bar.*)

AGNES. (*A savage look to* CLAIRE, *back to* EDNA.) She's coming home . . . I'm afraid.

EDNA. (*Disappointment.*) Oh . . . not again!

TOBIAS. (*Attempted levity.*) Just can't keep that one married, I guess.

EDNA. Oh, Agnes, what a shame!

HARRY. (*More embarrassed than sorry.*) Gee, that's too bad. (*Silence.*)

CLAIRE. Why *did* you come?

AGNES. Please! Claire! (*Back, reassuring.*) We're *glad* you're here; we're glad you came to surprise us!

TOBIAS. (*Quickly.*) Yes! (*Crosses to* CLAIRE, *hands her drink, then crosses to L. chair.*)

(HARRY *and* EDNA *exchange glances.*)

HARRY. (*Quite sad and curious about it.*) We were . . . sitting home . . . just sitting home. . . .

EDNA. Yes . . .

AGNES. (*Mildly reproving.*) We're *glad* to *see* you.

CLAIRE. (*Eyes narrowing, crossing R. of sofa.*) What happened, Harry?

AGNES. (*Sharp.*) Claire! Please!

TOBIAS. (*Wincing a little, shaking his head.*) Claire . . .

EDNA. (*Reassuring him.*) It's all right, Tobias.

AGNES. I don't see why people have to be questioned when they've come for a friendly . . .

CLAIRE. (*Small victory.*) Harry wants to tell you, Sis.

EDNA. Harry?

HARRY. We . . . well, we were sitting home . . .

TOBIAS. Can I get you a drink, Harry?

HARRY. (*Shakes his head.*) . . . I . . . we thought, about going to the club, but . . . it's, it's so crowded on a Friday night . . .

EDNA. (*Small voice, helpful, quiet.*) . . . with the canasta party, and getting ready for the dance to-morrow . . .

HARRY. . . . we didn't want to do that, and I've . . . been tired, and we didn't want to do that . . .

EDNA. . . . Harry's been tired this whole week.

HARRY. . . . so we had dinner home, and thought we'd stay . . .

EDNA. . . . rest.

AGNES. Of course.

CLAIRE. Shhhhh.

AGNES. (*Rather vicious.*) I WILL NOT SHHHH!

(CLAIRE *crosses* U. R. *on platform.*)

HARRY. Please? (*Waits a moment.*)

TOBIAS. (*Kind.*) Go on, Harry.

HARRY. So we were sitting, and Edna was doing that— that panel she works on. . . .

EDNA. (*Wistful, some loss.*) . . . my needlepoint . . .

HARRY. . . . and I was reading my French; I've got it pretty good now—not the accent, but the . . . the words. (*A brief silence.*)

CLAIRE. (*Quietly. Crosses to* R. *chair.*) And then?

HARRY. (*Looks over to her, a little dreamlike, as if he didn't know where he was.*) Hmm?

CLAIRE. (*Nicely.*) And then?

HARRY. (*Looks at* EDNA.) I . . . I don't know quite what happened then; we . . . we were . . . it was all very quiet, and we were all alone . . . (EDNA *begins to weep, quietly;* AGNES *notices, the others do not;* AGNES *does nothing.*) . . . and then . . . nothing happened,

but . . . (EDNA *is crying more openly now*.) . . . nothing
at all happened, but . . .

EDNA. (*Open weeping; loud.*) WE GOT . . . FRIGHT-
ENED. (*Open sobbing; no one moves.*)

HARRY. (*Quiet wonder, confusion.*) We got scared.

EDNA. (*Through her sobbing.*) WE WERE . . .
FRIGHTENED.

HARRY. There was nothing . . . but we were very
scared.

EDNA. We . . . were . . . terrified. (AGNES *crosses
to sofa, comforts* EDNA.)

HARRY. We were scared. (*Silence;* AGNES *comforting*
EDNA. HARRY *stock still. Quite innocent, almost child-
like.*) It was like being lost: very young again, with the
dark, and lost. There was no . . . thing . . . to be . . .
frightened of, but . . .

EDNA. (*Tears; quiet hysteria.*) WE WERE FRIGHT-
ENED . . . AND THERE WAS NOTHING. (*Silence
in the room.*)

HARRY. (*Matter-of-fact, but a hint of daring under it.*)
We couldn't stay there, and so we came here. You're our
very best friends.

EDNA. (*Crying softly now.*) In the whole world.

AGNES. (*Comforting, arms around her.*) Now, now,
Edna.

HARRY. (*Apologizing some.*) We couldn't go anywhere
else, so we came here.

AGNES. (*A deep breath, control.*) Well, we'll . . . you
did the right thing . . . of course.

TOBIAS. Sure.

EDNA. Can I go to bed now? Please?

AGNES. (*Pause; then, not quite understanding.*) Bed?

HARRY. We can't go back there.

EDNA. Please?

AGNES. (*Distant.*) Bed?

EDNA. (*Crosses U. R. of sofa.*) I'm so . . . tired.

HARRY. You're our best friends in the world. Tobias?

TOBIAS. (*A little bewilderment; rote.*) Of course we are, Harry.

EDNA. (*On her feet, moving.*) Please? (*Cries a little again.*)

AGNES. (*A million things going through her head, seeping through management.*) Of . . . of course you can. There's . . . there's Julia's room, and . . . (*Arm around* EDNA.) Come with me, dear. (HARRY *crosses to* C. *arch.* AGNES *reaches doorway; turns to* TOBIAS; *a question that has no answer.*) Tobias?

HARRY. (*Rises, begins to follow* EDNA, *rather automaton-like.*) Edna?

TOBIAS. (*Confused.*) Harry?

HARRY. (*Shaking his head.*) There was no one else we could go to.

(*He exits after* AGNES *and* EDNA. CLAIRE *sits up, watches* TOBIAS, *as he stands for a moment, looking at the floor: silence.*)

CLAIRE. (*A small, sad chuckle.*) I was wondering when it would begin . . . when it would start.

TOBIAS. (*Hearing her only after a moment.*) Start? (*Louder.*) START? (*Pause.*) WHAT?!

CLAIRE. (*Raises her glass to him.*) Don't you know yet? (*Small chuckle.*) You will.

CURTAIN

ACT TWO

Scene 1

Same set; before dinner, next evening, JULIA *and* AGNES
alone. AGNES *sitting, sofa* R., JULIA *on her feet, near*
L. *chair, pacing, maybe.*

JULIA. (*Anger and self-pity; too loud.*) Do you think
I like it? Do you?

AGNES. (*No pleading.*) Julia! Please!

JULIA. DO YOU! Do you think I enjoy it?

AGNES. Julia!

JULIA. Do you think it gives me some kind of . . .
martyr's pleasure? Do you?

AGNES. Will you be still?

JULIA. WELL!?

AGNES. THERE IS A HOUSE FULL OF PEOPLE!

JULIA. Yes! (*Crosses to* C. *arch.*) What *about* that! I
come home: my room is full of Harry and Edna. I have
no place to put my things. . . .

AGNES. (*Placating.*) They'll go to Tobias' room, he'll
sleep with me . . .

JULIA. (*Muttered.*) That'll be different.

AGNES. What did you say, young lady?

JULIA. (*Crosses to sofa* C.) I SAID, THAT WILL
BE NICE.

AGNES. You did *not* say any such thing. You said . . .

JULIA. (*Crosses to* R. *chair.*) What are they *doing* here?
Don't they have a house any more? Has the market gone
bust without my knowing it? I may have been out of
touch, but . . .

AGNES. Just . . . let it be.

JULIA. (*Between her teeth; controlled hysteria.*) Why
are they here?

33

AGNES. (*Weary; head back; calm.*) They're . . . frightened. Haven't you heard of it?

JULIA. (*Incredulous.*) They're . . . what!?

AGNES. (*Keeping her voice down.*) They're frightened. Now, will you let it be!

JULIA. (*Offended.*) What are they frightened of? Harry and *Edna*? Frightened?

AGNES. I don't . . . I don't know yet.

JULIA. Well, haven't you *talked* to them about it? I mean, for God's sake. . . .

AGNES. (*Trying to stay calm.*) No. I haven't.

JULIA. What have they done: stayed up in their room all day—*my* room!—not come down? Locked in?

AGNES. Yes.

JULIA. Yes what?

AGNES. Yes, they have stayed up in their room all day.

JULIA. My room.

AGNES. Your room. Now, let it be.

JULIA. (*Almost goes on in the same tone; doesn't; very nice, now.*) No, I . . .

AGNES. Please?

JULIA. (*Crosses to* R. *chair.*) I'm sorry, Mother, sorry for screeching.

AGNES. I am too old—as I remember—to remember what it is like to be a daughter, if my poor parents, in their separate heavens, will forgive me, but I am sure it is simpler than being a mother.

JULIA. (*Slight edge.*) I said I was sorry.

AGNES. (*All of this more for her own bemusement and amusement than anything else.*) I don't recall if I ever asked my poor mother that. I do wish sometimes that I had been born a man.

JULIA. (*Shakes her head; very matter-of-fact.*) Not so hot.

AGNES. Their concerns are so simple: money and death—making ends meet until they meet the end. (*Great self-mockery and exaggeration.*) If they *knew* what it was like . . . to be a wife; a mother; a lover; a home

maker; a nurse; a hostess, an agitator, a pacifier, a truth-
teller, a deceiver . . .

JULIA. (*Saws away at an invisible violin; sings.*) Da-
da-dee; da-da-da.

AGNES. (*Laughs softly.*) There is a book out, I believe,
a new one by one of the thirty million psychiatrists
practicing in this land of ours, a book which opines that
the sexes are reversing, or coming to resemble each other
too much, at any rate. It is a book to be read and dis-
believed, for it disturbs our sense of well-being. If the
book is right, and I suspect it is, then I would be no
better off as a man . . . would I?

JULIA. (*Sober, though tongue-in-cheek agreement;
shaking of head.*) No. Not at all.

AGNES. (*Exaggerated fret. Crosses to* R. *chair.*) Oh!
There is nowhere to rest the weary head . . . or whatever. (*Hand out; loving, though a little grand.*) How are
you, my darling?

JULIA. (*A little abrupt. Moves hand away.*) What?

AGNES. (*Hand still out; somewhat strained.*) How are
you, my darling?

JULIA. (*Gathering energy.*) How is your darling?
(*Crosses to* L. *of sofa.*) Well, I was trying to tell you
before you shut me up with Harry and Edna hiding upstairs, and . . .

AGNES. ALL RIGHT! (*Crosses to platform.*)

(*A pause.*)

JULIA. (*Strained control. Crosses to* AGNES.) I will try
to tell you, Mother—once again—before you've turned
into a man . . .

AGNES. I shall try to hear you out, but if I feel my
voice changing, in the middle of your . . . rant, you will
have to forgive my male prerogative, if I become uncomfortable, look at my watch, or jiggle the change in
my pocket . . . (*Sees* JULIA *marching toward the archway as* TOBIAS *enters. Crosses* U. R. *of arch.*) . . . where
do you think you're going?

JULIA. (*Head down, muttered.*) . . . you go straight to hell. . . .

TOBIAS. (*Attempt at cheer.*) Now, now, what's going on here? (*At arch* C.)

JULIA. (*Right in front of him; force.*) Will you shut her up?

TOBIAS. (*Overwhelmed.*) Will I . . . what?

AGNES. (*Marching toward the archway herself.*) Well, there you are, Julia; your father may safely leave the room now, I think. Hello, my darling. (*Back to* JULIA.) Your mother has arrived. Talk to *him!* (*To* TOBIAS.) Your daughter is in need of consolation or a great cuffing around the ears. I don't know which to recommend.

TOBIAS. (*Steps* L. *Confused.*) Have . . . have Harry and Edna . . . ?

AGNES. (*Exiting.*) No, they have not. (*Gone.*)

TOBIAS. (*After her, vaguely.*) Well, I thought maybe . . . (*To* JULIA, *rather timid.*) What was that . . . all about?

JULIA. As they say: I haven't the faintest.

TOBIAS. (*Willing to let it go.*) Oh. (*Crosses to* U. C.)

JULIA. (*Rather brittle.*) Evening papers? (*Crosses* C.)

TOBIAS. Oh, yes; want them?

JULIA. Anything happy?

TOBIAS. (*Hopefully.*) My daughter's home. (*Crosses to* JULIA, *kisses her on cheek.*)

JULIA. (*Not giving in.*) Any other joys? (*Crosses* D. R.)

TOBIAS. Sorry. (*Crosses to* D. L. *chair. Sighs.*) No: small wars, large anxieties, our dear Republicans as dull as ever, a teen-age marijuana nest not far from here . . . (*Some wonder.*) I've never had marijuana . . . in my entire life.

JULIA. Want some?

TOBIAS. Wasn't fashionable.

JULIA. (*Crosses to* R. *chair.*) What the hell do Harry and Edna want?

TOBIAS. (*Scratches his head.*) Just let it be.

JULIA. (*Crosses* U. R. *of sofa.*) Didn't you try to talk to them today? I mean . . .

TOBIAS. (*Not embarrassed, but not comfortable either.*) Well, no; they weren't down when I went off to the club, and . . .

JULIA. Good old golf?

TOBIAS. (*Surprisingly nasty.*) Don't ride me, Julia, I warn you. (*Crosses* U. L.)

JULIA. (*Nervously nicer. Crosses to* TOBIAS.) I've never had any marijuana, either. Aren't I a good old girl?

TOBIAS. (*Thinking of something else.*) Either that or slow.

JULIA. (*Exploding; but anger, not hysteria. Crosses to* R. *chair.*) Great Christ! What the hell did I come home to? And why? Both of you? Snotty, mean . . .

TOBIAS. (*Crossing to her.*) LOOK! (*Silence; softer, but no nonsense.*) There are some . . . times, when it all gathers up . . . too much.

JULIA. (*Nervously.*) Sure, sure.

TOBIAS. (*Not put off.*) Some *times* when it's going to be Agnes and Tobias, and not just Mother and Dad. Right? (*Crosses to* C.) Some *times* when the allowances aren't going to me made. What are you doing, biting off your fingernails now?

JULIA. (*Not giving in.*) It broke off.

TOBIAS. (*Crosses to* U. R.) There are some *times* when it's all . . . too much. *I* don't know what the hell Harry and Edna are doing sitting up in that bedroom! (*Crosses to* D. R.) Claire is drinking, she and Agnes are at each other like a couple of . . . of . . .

JULIA. (*Softly.*) Sisters?

TOBIAS. (*Crosses to* R. *chair.*) What? The goddamn government's at me over some deductions, and you!

JULIA. (*Head high, defiant.*) And me? Yes?

TOBIAS. (*Crosses to* U. C.) This isn't the first time, you know. This isn't the first time you've come back with one of your goddamned marriages on the rocks. Four! Count 'em!

JULIA. (*Rage.*) I know how many marriages I've gotten myself into, you . . .

TOBIAS. Four! You expect to come back here, nestle in to being fifteen and misunderstood each time? You are thirty-six years old, for God's sake! . . .

JULIA. And you are one hundred! Easily!

TOBIAS. Thirty-six! Each time! Dragging your . . . your—I was going to say pride—your marriage with you like some Raggedy Ann doll, by the foot. (*Crosses to R. of sofa.*) You, you fill this house with your whining. . . .

JULIA. (*Rage. Crosses to C. sofa.*) I DON'T ASK TO COME BACK HERE!!

TOBIAS. (*Steps in to* JULIA.) YOU BELONG HERE! (*Heavy breathing from both of them, finally a little rueful giggle;* TOBIAS *speaks rather nonchalantly now.* TOBIAS *crosses to* JULIA.) Well. Now that I've taken out on my only daughter the . . . disgust of my declining years, I'll mix a very good and very strong martini. Join me? (*Crosses to bar, mixes martini.*)

JULIA. (*Rather wistful.*) When I was a very little girl— well, when I was a little girl: after I'd gotten over my two-year burn at suddenly having a brother, may his soul rest, when I was still a little girl, I thought you were a marvel—saint, sage, daddy, everything. And then, as the years turned and I reached my . . . somewhat angular adolescence.

TOBIAS. (*At the sideboard; unconcerned.*) Five to one? Or more?

JULIA. And then as the years turned—poor old man— you sank to cipher, and you've stayed there, I'm afraid— very nice but ineffectual, essential, but not-really-thought- of, gray . . . non-eminence.

TOBIAS. (*Mixing, hardly listening.*) Unh-hunh . . .

JULIA. And now you've changed again, sea monster, ram! Nasty, violent, absolutely human man! Yes, as you make it, five to one, or better.

TOBIAS. I made it about seven, I think.

JULIA. Your transformations amaze me. How can I

have changed so much? Or *is* it really you? (*Crosses to*
JULIA. *He hands her a drink.*) Thank you. (JULIA *slides
to sofa* C.)

TOBIAS. (*Sits* R. *on sofa. As they* BOTH *settle.*) I told
Agnes that I'd speak to Doug . . . if you think that
would do any good. By golly, Dad, that's a good martini!

JULIA. Do you really want to talk to Doug? You won't
get anywhere: the compulsives you can get somewhere
with—or the illusion of getting—the gamblers, the fags,
the lechers . . .

TOBIAS. . . . of this world . . .

JULIA. . . . yes, you can have the illusion 'cause
they're after something, the jackpot, somehow: break the
bank, find the boy, climb the babe . . . something.

TOBIAS. You do pick'em.

JULIA. (*Pregnant.*) *Do* I?

TOBIAS. Hm?

JULIA. *Do* I pick 'em? I thought it was fifteen hundred
and six, or so, where daughter went with whatever man
her parents thought would hold the fief together best,
or something. "Love will come after."

TOBIAS. (*Grudging.*) Well, you may have been pushed
on Charlie . . .

JULIA. Poor Charlie.

TOBIAS. (*Temper rising a little.*) Well, for Christ's sake,
if you miss him so much . . .

JULIA. I do not miss him! Well, yes, I do, but not that
way. Because he seemed so like what Teddy would have
been.

TOBIAS. (*Quiet anger and sorrow.*) Your brother would
not have grown up to be a fag.

JULIA. (*Bitter smile.*) Who is to say?

TOBIAS. (*Hard look.*) I! (*Pause.* CLAIRE *in the archway.*)

CLAIRE. Do I breathe gin? (JULIA *sees her, rises, runs
to her, arms out,* BOTH *of them, they envelop each other.*)
Darling!

JULIA. Oh, my sweet Claire!

CLAIRE. Julia Julia. (*They cross* D. R.)

JULIA. (*Semi-mock condemnation.*) I must say the welcome-home committee was pretty skimpy, you and Daddy gone. . . .

CLAIRE. Oh, now. (*To* TOBIAS.) I said, do I breathe gin?

TOBIAS. (*Not rising.*) You do.

CLAIRE. (*Appraising* JULIA.) Well, you don't look too bad for a quadruple amputee, I must say. (*Crosses to sofa.*) Are you going to make me a whatever, Tobias? (*To* JULIA.) Besides, my darling, it's getting to be rather a habit, isn't it?

JULIA. (*False smile.*) Yes, I suppose so.

CLAIRE. (*Sees* TOBIAS *is not moving.*) Then I shall make my own.

TOBIAS. (*Getting up; wearily. Crosses to bar.*) Sit down, Claire, I'll do it.

CLAIRE. (*Steps* L..) I wouldn't want to tax you, now. (*Generally.*) Well, I had an adventure today. Went into town, thought I'd shake 'em up a little, so I tried to find me a topless bathing suit.

JULIA. (*Giggling, crosses to* R. *chair.*) You didn't!

TOBIAS. (*At the sideboard, disapproving.*) Really, Claire.

CLAIRE. (*At bar.*) Yes, I did. I went into what's-their-names', and I went straight up to the swim-wear, as they call it, department and I got me an eighteen-nineties schoolteacher type, who wondered what she could do for me. (JULIA *giggles.*) And I felt like telling her, "Not much, sweetheart" . . .

TOBIAS. (*Steps in with bottle of Pepsi Cola.*) Are you sure you wouldn't rather have a . . .

CLAIRE. Very. (TOBIAS *steps back to bar, continues martini mixing.*) But I said, "Hello, there, I'm in the market for a topless swimsuit."

JULIA. You know! They *are* wearing them on the coast. I've . . .

CLAIRE. Hush. Hurry up there, Toby. "A what, Miss?" she said, which I didn't know whether to take as a compliment or not. "A topless swimsuit," I said. "I don't know what you mean," she said after a beat. "Oh, certainly you do," I said, "no top, stops at the waist, latest thing, lots of freedom." "Oh, yes," she said, looking at me like she was seeing the local madam for the first time, "those." Then a real sniff. "I'm afraid we don't carry . . . those."

JULIA. (*Crosses to sofa,* R. *arm.*) I could have brought you one! . . . (*Afterthought.*) If I'd known I was coming home.

CLAIRE. "Well, in that case," I told her, "do you have any separates?" "Those we carry," she said, "those we do." And she started going under the counter, and I said, "I'll just buy the bottoms of one of those."

JULIA. No! You didn't!

CLAIRE. Yes, I did. She came up from under the counter, adjusted her spectacles and said, "What did you say?"

TOBIAS. Shall I bring it, or will you come for it?

CLAIRE. You bring. I said, "I said, 'I'll buy the bottom of one of those.'" She thought for a minute, and then she said, with ice in her voice, "And what will we do with the tops?" "Well," I said, "why don't you save 'em? Maybe bottomless swimsuits'll be in *next* year." (JULIA *laughs openly.*) Then the poor sweet thing gave me a look I couldn't tell was either a D-minus, or she was going to send me home with a letter to my mother, and she said, sort of far away, "I think you need the manager." And off she walked.

TOBIAS. (*Crosses to* CLAIRE. *Handing* CLAIRE *her martini; mildly amused throughout.*) What were you doing buying a bathing suit in October, anyway?

JULIA. (*Crosses to* R. *chair.*) Oh, Dad!

CLAIRE. No, now; it's a man's question. (*Sips.*) Wow, what a good martini.

TOBIAS. (*Still standing over her, rather severe.*) Truth will get you nowhere. Why?

CLAIRE. Why? Well . . . (*Thinks.*) . . . maybe I'll go on a trip somewhere.

TOBIAS. That would please Agnes. (*Crosses to* D. L. *chair.*)

CLAIRE. (*Nods.*) As few things would. What I meant was, maybe Toby'll walk in one day, trailing travel folders, rip his tie off, announce he's fed up to there with the north, the east, the suburbs, the regulated great gray life, dwindling before him—poor Toby—and has bought him an island off Paraguay . . .

TOBIAS. . . . which has no seacoast . . .

CLIARE. . . . yes, *way* off—has bought him this island, and is taking us all to *that,* to hack through the whatever, build us an enormous leanto, all of us. Take us away, to where it is always good and happy. (*Watches* TOBIAS, *who looks at his drink, frowning a little.*)

JULIA. (*She, too, crossing* L.) Would you, Dad?

TOBIAS. (*Looks up, sees them* BOTH *looking at him, frowns more.*) It's . . . it's too late, or something.

(*Small silence.*)

CLAIRE. (*To lighten it.*) Or, maybe I simply wanted a topless bathing suit. (*Pause.*) No? Well, then . . . maybe it's more complicated yet. I mean, Claire couldn't find herself a man if she tried, and here comes Julia, home from the wars. . . .

TOBIAS. (*Quiet contradiction.*) You could find a man.

CLAIRE. (*Some bitterness.*) Indeed, I have found several, briefly, and none my own.

TOBIAS. (*To* JULIA; *terribly offhand.*) Don't you think Auntie Claire could find herself a man?

JULIA. (*Didactic.*) I *don't* like the subject.

CLAIRE. . . . and here comes Julia, home from the wars, four purple hearts . . .

JULIA. (*Crosses* U. R.) Why don't you just have another drink and stop it, Claire?

CLAIRE. (*Looks at her empty glass, shrugs.*) All right.

JULIA. (*Rather defensive.*) I have *left* Doug. We are not *divorced*.

CLAIRE. Yet! Are you cooking a second batch, Tobias? (*Back to* JULIA.) But you've come back home, haven't you? And didn't you—with the others?

JULIA. (*Her back up.*) Where else am I supposed to go?

CLAIRE. It's a great big world, baby. There are hotels, new cities. Home is the quickest road to Reno I know of.

JULIA. (*Condescending, crossing to* R. *of sofa.*) You've had a lot of experience in these matters, Claire.

CLAIRE. Sidelines! Good seats, right on the fifty-yard line, objective observer. (*Texas accent, or near it.*) I swar! Ef I din't love muh sister so, Ah'd say she got yuh hitched fur the pleasure uh gettin' yuh back.

JULIA. ALL RIGHT!	TOBIAS. THAT WILL
(*Turns away.*)	DO NOW! (*He crosses to bar.*)

CLAIRE. (*In the silence that follows.*) Sorry. Very . . . very sorry.

(AGNES *appears through the archway.*)

AGNES. (*What she may have overheard she gives no indication of.*) "They" tell me in the kitchen . . . "they" tell me we are about to dine. In a bit. Are we having a cocktail? I think one might be nice. (*Puts her arm around* JULIA *as she passes her.*) It's one of those days when everything's underneath. But, we are all together . . . which is something.

JULIA. Quite a few of us. (*Crosses* U. R.)

TOBIAS. Any word from . . . (*Points to the ceiling.*) . . . up there?

AGNES. (*Crosses to* L. *chair.*) No. I dropped upstairs—well, *that* doesn't make very much sense, does it?—I *happened* upstairs, and I knocked at Harry and Edna's *Julia's* room, door, and after a moment I heard Harry

say, "It's all right; we're all right." I didn't have the . . .
well, I felt such an odd mixture of . . . embarrassment
and irritation, and . . . apprehension, I suppose, and . . .
fatigue . . . I didn't persevere.

TOBIAS. (*Steps in.*) Well, haven't they been *out?* I
mean, haven't they eaten or anything? (*Crosses to bar.*)

AGNES. Will you make me a . . . thing, a martini,
please? I am told—"*they*" tell me that while we were all
out, at our various whatever-they-may-be's, Edna de-
scended, asked them to make sandwiches, which were
brought to the closed door and handed in.

TOBIAS. (*Steps in.*) Well, God, I mean . . .

AGNES. (*Rather a recitation.*) There is no point in
pressing it, they are our very dear friends, they will tell
us in good time.

CLAIRE. (*Looking through her glass.*) I had a glimmer
of it last night; thought I knew.

AGNES. (*So gracious.*) That which we see in the bottom
of our glass is most often dregs.

CLAIRE. (*Peers into her glass, over-curious.*) Really?
Truly so?

TOBIAS. (*Holding a glass out to* AGNES.) Did you say
you wanted?

AGNES. (*Her eyes still on* CLAIRE.) Yes, I did, thank
you.

(TOBIAS *crosses to bar, pours martini.*)

CLAIRE. We have been trying, your husband and I,
without very much success, to find out why Miss Julie
here is come home.

AGNES. I would imagine Julia is home because she
wishes to be, and it is where she belongs if she wants.

(JULIA *crosses to* R.)

TOBIAS. (*Crossing to* AGNES.) That's logistics, isn't it?
(*Hands her martini.*)

AGNES. You too?

(TOBIAS *crosses* U. R.)

JULIA. He's against everything!

AGNES. Your father?

JULIA. Doug!

AGNES. You needn't make a circus of it; tell me later, when . . .

JULIA. (*Crossing* U. L.) War, marriage, money, children . . .

AGNES. You needn't!

JULIA. You! Daddy! Government! Claire—if he'd met her . . . everything!

CLAIRE. (*Lies on sofa.*) Well, I doubt he'd dislike *me;* I'm against everything too.

AGNES. (*To* JULIA.) You're tired; we'll talk about it after . . .

JULIA. (*Sick disgust.*) I've talked about it! I just talked about it!

AGNES. (*Quiet boring in.*) I'm sure there's more.

JULIA. There is no more. (*Crosses to bar, puts down her glass.*)

AGNES. (*Clenched teeth.*) There is a great deal more, and I'll hear it from you later, when we're alone. You have not come to us in your fourth debacle . . .

JULIA. (*At bar.*) HE IS OPPOSED! AND THAT IS ALL! TO EVERYTHING!

AGNES. (*After a small silence.*) Perhaps after dinner.

JULIA. (*Crosses Downstage of* AGNES.) NO! NOT PERHAPS AFTER DINNER!

TOBIAS. ALL OF YOU! BE STILL! (*Silence.*)

CLAIRE. (*Flat; to* TOBIAS.) Are we having our dividend, or are we not? (CLAIRE *sits up,* TOBIAS *crosses to* L. *chair.* JULIA *crosses* U. L. *Silence; then, a gentle mocking apology.*) "All happy families are alike."

(HARRY *and* EDNA *appear in the archway, coats on or over arms.*)

HARRY. (*A little embarrassed.*) Well.

CLAIRE. (*Exaggerated bonhomie.*) Well, look who's here!

TOBIAS. (*Embarrassed, crossing* U. L.) Harry, just in time for a martini. . . .

HARRY. No, no, we're . . . Julia, there you are!

EDNA. (*Affectionate commiseration.*) Oh, Julia.

JULIA. (*Bravely, nicely.*) Hello there.

AGNES. (*On her feet.*) There's just time for a drink before dinner, if my husband will hurry some . . .

(TOBIAS *steps to bar.*)

HARRY. No, we're . . . going home now.

AGNES. (*Relief peeking through the surprise.*) Oh? Yes?

EDNA. Yes. (*Pause.*)

AGNES. (*Crosses* U. L.) Well. (*Pause.*) If we were any help at all, we . . .

HARRY. To . . . uh, to get our things. (*Silence.*) Our clothes, and things.

EDNA. Yes.

HARRY. We'll be back in . . . well, after dinner, so don't . . .

EDNA. An hour or two. It'll take us a while.

(*Silence.* AGNES *begins to cross to arch.*)

HARRY. We'll let ourselves . . . don't bother.

(*They start out, tentatively, see that the others are merely staring at them. They exit. Silence.*)

JULIA. (*Controlled, but near tears.*) I want my room back! I want my room!

AGNES. (*Composed, chilly, standing in the archway.*) I believe that dinner is served. . . .

TOBIAS. (*Vacant.*) Yes?

AGNES. If any of you have the stomach for it.

CURTAIN

ACT TWO

Scene 2

Same set, after dinner, the same evening. Julia *seated on sofa* L. Tobias *standing near* L. *chair.* Agnes *standing at windows.*

Julia. (*A statement, directed to neither of them.*) That was, without question, the *ugliest* dinner I have ever sat through.

Agnes. (*Seemingly pleased. Turns in.*) What did you say? (*No answer. Steps* L. C.) Now, what can you mean? Was the ragout not to your pleasure? Did the floating island sink? Watch what you say, for your father is proud of his wines. . . . (*Turns* R.)

Julia. No! You! Sitting there! Like a combination . . . pope, and . . . "We will not discuss it"; "Claire, be still"; "No, Tobias, the table is not the proper place"; "Julia!" . . . nanny! Like a nanny!

Agnes. (*Crosses to* U. R. *sofa.*) When we are dealing with children . . .

Julia. I must discover, sometime, who you think you are.

Agnes. (*Icy.*) You will learn . . . one day.

Julia. No, more like a drill sergeant! *You* will do this, *you* will not say that.

Agnes. "To keep in shape." Have you heard the expression? Most people misunderstand it, assume it means alteration, when it does not. Maintenance. When we keep something in shape, we maintain its shape— whether we are proud of that shape, or not, is another matter—we keep *it* from falling apart. We do not attempt the impossible. We maintain. We hold.

Julia. Yes? So?

Agnes. (*Quietly.*) I shall . . . keep this family in shape. I shall maintain it; hold it.

JULIA. (*A sneer.*) But you won't attempt the impossible.

AGNES. (*A smile.*) I shall keep it in shape. If I am a drill sergeant . . . so be it. Since nobody . . . *really* wants to talk about your latest . . . marital disorder, really wants to talk *around* it, use it as an excuse for all sorts of horrid little revenges . . . I think we can at least keep the table . . . unlittered of *that*.

JULIA. (*Sarcastic salute, not rising though.*) Yes, sir.

AGNES. (*Reasonable.*) And, if I shout, it's merely to be heard . . . above the awful din of your privacies and sulks . . . all of you. I am not being an ogre, am I?

TOBIAS. (*Not anxious to argue. Crosses to* D. R. *window.*) No, no; very . . . reasonable.

AGNES. If I am a stickler on certain points (*Just as* JULIA's *mouth opens* to speak.) —a martinet, as Julia would have it, would you not, sweet?, in fact, were you not about to?—if I am a stickler on points of manners, timing, tact—the graces, I almost blush to call them— it is simply that I am the one membei of this . . . reasonably happy family blessed and burdened with the ability to view a situation objectively while I am in it.

JULIA. (*Not really caring. Rises, crossing to* D. L. *chair.*) What time is it?

AGNES. (*A little harder now.*) The double position of seeing not only facts but their implications . . .

TOBIAS. (*Facing off* R.) Nearly ten.

AGNES. (*Some irritation toward both of them.*) . . . the longer view as well as the shorter. There *is* a balance to be maintained, after all, though the rest of you teeter, unconcerned, or uncaring, *assuming* you're on level ground . . . by divine right, I gather, though that is hardly so. And if I must be the fulcrum . . . (*Sees neither of them is really listening, says in the same tone.*) . . . I think I shall have a divorce. (*Smiles to see that her words have had no effect. Crosses to* R. *of sofa.*)

TOBIAS. (*It sinks in. Steps in.*) Have what? A *what?*

AGNES. No fear; merely testing. Everything is taken for granted and no one listens.

TOBIAS. (*Wrinkling his nose, crossing to* R. *chair.*) Have a divorce? (*Sits.*)

AGNES. No, no; Julia has them for all of us. Not even separation; that is taken care of, and in life: the gradual . . . demise of intensity, the private preoccupations, the substitutions. We become allegorical, my darling Tobias, as we grow older. The individuality we hold so dearly sinks into crotchet; we see ourselves repeated by those we bring into it all, either by mirror or rejection, honor or fault. (*To herself, really.*) I'm not a fool; I'm really not.

JULIA. (*Leafing a magazine; clear lack of interest but not insulting.*) What's Claire up to?

AGNES. (*Walking to* TOBIAS, *a hand on his shoulder.*) Really not at all.

TOBIAS. (*Looking up; fondness.*) No; really not.

AGNES. (*Surprisingly unfriendly; to* JULIA.) How would I know what she's doing?

JULIA. (*She too. Crosses* U. R.) Well, you are the fulcrum and all around here, the double vision, the great balancing act . . . (*Lets it slide away.*)

AGNES. (*A little triste; looking away.*) I dare say she's in her room.

JULIA. (*Little girl.*) At least she has one.

AGNES. (*Swinging around to face her; quite hard.*) Well, why don't you run upstairs and claim your goddamn room back! (JULIA *crosses* D. R. TOBIAS *rises, crosses to* D. L. *chair.*) Barricade yourself in there! Push a bureau in front of the door! Take Tobias' pistol while you're at it! Arm yourself!

(*A burst from an* ACCORDION; CLAIRE *appears in the archway, wearing it.*)

CLAIRE. Barricades? Pistols? Really? So soon?

JULIA. (*Giggling in spite of herself.*) Oh, Claire . . .

AGNES. (*Not amused.*) Claire, will you take off that damned thing!

CLAIRE. (*Crosses to sofa, sits on back.*) "They laughed when I sat down to the accordion." Take it off? No, I will not! This is going to be a festive night—from the smell of it, and sister Claire wants to do her part—pay her way, so to speak . . . justify.

AGNES. You're not going to play that dreadful instrument in here, and . . . (*But the rest of what she wants to say is drowned out by a chord from the ACCORDION.*) Tobias? (*Calm.*) Do something about that.

TOBIAS. (*He, too, chuckling.*) Oh, now, Agnes . . .

CLAIRE. So . . . (*Crosses* U. R. *of sofa. Another chord.*) . . . shall I wait? Shall I start now? A polka? What?

AGNES. (*Icy, but to* TOBIAS.) My sister is not *really* lazy. The things she has learned since leaving the nest!: gaucherie, ingratitude, drunkenness, and even . . . this. She has become a musician, too.

CLAIRE. (*A twang in her voice.*) Maw used to say: "Claire, girl" . . . she had an uncle named Claire, so she always called me Claire-girl—

AGNES. (*No patience with it.*) That is not so.

CLAIRE. (*At* U. C.) "Claire girl," she used to say, "when you go out into the world, get dumped outa the nest, or pushed by your sister . . ."

AGNES. (*Steady, but burning. At* L. *of sofa.*) Lies. (*Eyes slits.*) She kept you, allowed you . . . tolerated! Put up with your filth, your . . . "emancipated womanhood." (*To* JULIA, *overly sweet.*) Even in her teens, your Auntie Claire had her own and very special ways, was very . . . advanced.

CLAIRE. (*Laughs.*) Had a ball, the same as you, 'cept I wasn't puce with socially proper remorse every time. (*To* JULIA, *crossing to sofa, at* L. *arm.*) Your mommy got her pudenda scuffed a couple times herself 'fore she met old Toby, you know.

TOBIAS. Your what?

AGNES. (*Majesty.*) My pudenda.

(TOBIAS *rises, crosses* U. L.)

CLAIRE. (*A little grumpy.*) You can come on all forgetful in your old age, if you want to, but just remember . . .

AGNES. (*Quiet anger. Crosses to sofa.*) I am not an old woman. (*Sudden thought; to* TOBIAS.) Am I?

TOBIAS. (*No help; great golly-gosh.*) Well, you're my old lady . . .

(AGNES *almost says something, changes her mind.*)

CLAIRE. (*A chord. Crosses* U. C.) Well, what'll it be?

JULIA. (*Glum.*) Save it for Harry and Edna.

CLAIRE. (*Crosses to* L.) Save it for Harry and Edna? Save it for them? (*Chord.*)

AGNES. (*Nice.*) Please.

CLAIRE. (*Crosses to* D. L. *chair.*) All right; I'll unload. (*Removes ACCORDION.*)

AGNES. I dare say . . . (*Stops.*)

TOBIAS. (*Crossing* U. R.) What?

AGNES. No. Nothing.

CLAIRE. (*Half-smile.*) We're waiting, aren't we?

TOBIAS. Hm?

CLAIRE. (*Crosses to sofa.*) Waiting. The room; the doctor's office; beautiful unconcern; intensive study of the dreadful curtains; absorption in *Field and Stream,* waiting for the Bi-op-*see.* (*Looks from one to the other.*) No? Don't know what I mean?

JULIA. (*Rather defiant. Crosses* U. R. *of sofa.*) What *about* Harry and Edna?

CLAIRE. (*Echo; half-smile. Crosses to* L. *of chair.*) We don't want to talk about it.

AGNES. *If* they come back . . .

CLAIRE. *If!?*

AGNES. (*Closes her eyes briefly. Crosses* R.) If they come back . . . we will . . . (*Shrugs.*)

CLAIRE. You've only got two choices, Sis. You take 'em in, or you throw 'em out.

AGNES. (*Stops.*) An, how simple it is from the side-lines. (*Crosses to windows.*)

TOBIAS. (*Crosses sofa.*) We'll do neither, I'd imagine. Take in; throw out.

CLAIRE. Oh?

TOBIAS. (*A feeling of nakedness.*) Well, yes, they're just . . . passing through.

CLAIRE. As they have been . . . all these years.

AGNES. Well, we shall know soon enough. (*Not too much pleasure.*) They're back.

TOBIAS. Yes?

JULIA. (*Crosses U. C.*) I think I'll go up . . .

AGNES. You stay right here!

JULIA. I want to go to my . . .

AGNES. It is their room! For the moment.

JULIA. (*Not nice. Crosses to* AGNES.) Among Doug's opinions, you might like to know, is that when you and your ilk are blown to pieces by a Chinese bomb, the world will be a better place.

CLAIRE. (*Crosses to* L. *chair.*) Isn't ilk a lovely word?

TOBIAS. (*Disbelief.*) Oh, come on now! (*Crosses, slaps* JULIA's *fanny; then crosses to arch and exits to* R.)

CLAIRE. It will certainly be a less crowded one.

AGNES. (*Dry.*) You choose well, Julia.

JULIA. (*Retreating into uncertainty.*) That's what he says. (*Crosses to* R. *arm of sofa.*)

AGNES. (*On platform* U. R.) Have, always. Did he include *you* as ilk, as well? Will you be with us when "the fatal mushroom" comes, as those dirty boys put it? Are we to have the pleasure?

JULIA. (*After a pause; as much a threat as a promise.*) I'll be right here.

TOBIAS. (*He enters* U. C.) Agnes!

JULIA. (*Crosses to* AGNES.) Would you like to know something else he says?

AGNES. (*Patiently.*) No, Julia. (*Turns away.*)

JULIA. Dad?

TOBIAS. (*Some apology in it.*) Not . . . right this minute, Julia. (*Exits.*)

JULIA. (*Defiance. Crosses to* L. *chair.*) Claire? You?

CLAIRE. (*Crossing to coffee table, picking up tray with demitasse service, crossing* U. L. *with it and leaving it on table.*) Well, come on! You *know* I'd like to hear about it—love to—but Toby and Ag've got an invasion on their hands, and . . .

AGNES. We have no such thing. (*Crosses* U. C.)

CLAIRE. . . . maybe you'd better save it for Harry and Edna, too.

AGNES. It does not concern Harry and Edna.

CLAIRE. Best friends.

AGNES. Tobias?

TOBIAS. (*Enters.*) Where . . . what do you want me to do with everything? Every . . . ?

(JULIA *crosses to sofa.*)

AGNES. Well for God's sake! I'll do it. (*They exit.*)

JULIA. (*As* CLAIRE *moves to the bar.*) What . . . what do they want? Harry and Edna.

CLAIRE. (*Pouring brandy for herself.*) Hmm?

JULIA. You'll make Mother mad. Harry and Edna: what do they want?

CLAIRE. Succor.

JULIA. (*Tiny pause.*) Pardon?

CLAIRE. (*Brief smile.*) Comfort. (*Sees* JULIA *doesn't understand. Crosses to* L. *of sofa.*) Warmth. A special room with a night light, or the door ajar so you can look down the hall from the bed and see that Mommy's door is open.

JULIA. (*No anger; loss.*) But that's my room.

CLAIRE. (*Crosses* U. C. *of sofa.*) It's . . . the *room.* Happens you were in it. You're a visitor as much as anyone, now. (*We hear mumbled conversation from the hallway.*)

JULIA. (*Small whine.*) But I *know* that room.

CLAIRE. (*Pointed, but kind. Crosses to* R. *of sofa.*) Are you home for good now? (JULIA *stares at her.*) Are you home forever, back from the world? To the sadness *and* reassurance of your parents? Have you come to take my place?

JULIA. (*Quiet despair. Crosses to* L. *chair.*) This is my home!

CLAIRE. This . . . ramble? Yes? (*Surprised delight.*) You're laying claim to the cave! Well, I don't know how they'll take to that. We're not a communal nation, dear; (*Crosses* U. L. *of sofa.* EDNA *appears in the archway, unseen.*) giving, but not sharing, outgoing, but not friendly.

EDNA. Hello.

CLAIRE. (*Friendly, but not turning to look at her.*) Hello! (*Back to* JULIA.) We submerge our truths and have our sunsets on untroubled waters. C'mon in, Edna.

EDNA. Yes.

CLAIRE. (*Back to* JULIA.) We live with our truths in the grassy bottom, and we examine aallll the interpretations of aalllll the implications like we had a life for nothing else, for God's sake. (*Crosses to* EDNA *at arch.*) Do *you think* we can walk on the water, Edna? Or do you think we sink?

EDNA. (*Dry.*) We sink.

CLAIRE. And we better develop gills. Right?

EDNA. Right.

(EDNA *crosses* D. R. *of sofa;* CLAIRE U. L. *of sofa.*)

JULIA. I didn't see you come in.

EDNA. We drove around the back. Harry is helping Agnes and Tobias get our bags upstairs.

JULIA. (*Slight schoolteacher tone.*) Don't you mean Agnes and Tobias are helping Harry?

EDNA. (*Tired.*) If you like. (*To* CLAIRE.) What were you two up to?

CLAIRE. (*Crosses to* L. *chair.*) I think Julia is home for good this time.

JULIA. (*Annoyed and embarrassed.*) For Christ's sake, Claire!

EDNA. (*Rather as if* JULIA *were not in the room.*) Oh? Is it come to that?

CLAIRE. I always said she would, finally.

JULIA. (*Under her breath, to* CLAIRE, *crossing* U. L.) This is family business!

EDNA. (*Looking around the room.*) Yes, but I'm not sure Agnes and Tobias have seen it as clearly. I do wish Agnes would have that chair recovered. Perhaps now . . .

JULIA. (*Exploding. Crosses* D. R. *of* R. *chair.*) Well, why don't you call the upholsterers! Now that you're living here!

CLAIRE. (*Quiet amusement.*) All in the family.

EDNA. You're not a child any more, Julia, you're nicely on your way to forty, and you've not helped . . . wedlock's image any, with your . . . shenanigans . . .

JULIA. (*Full, quivering rage.*) YOU ARE A GUEST IN THIS HOUSE!!

EDNA. (*Lets a moment pass, continues quietly.*) . . . and if you *have* decided to . . . (*Wistful.*) return forever? . . . then it's a matter of some concern for quite a few peo—

JULIA. You are a *guest!*

CLAIRE. (*Quietly.*) As you.

EDNA. . . . for quite a few people . . . whose lives are . . . moved—if not necessarily touched—by your actions. Claire, where does Agnes have her upholstery done? Does she use . . .

JULIA. NO!

EDNA. (*Strict, soft and powerful.*) Manners, young lady!

CLAIRE. (*Pointed.*) Julia, why don't you ask Edna if she'd like something?

JULIA. (*Mouth agape for a moment.*) NO! (*To* EDNA.) You have no rights here. . . .

EDNA. I'll have a cognac, Julia. (EDNA *continues; precise and pointed*.) My husband and I are your parents' best friends. We are, in addition, your godparents.

JULIA. DOES THIS GIVE YOU RIGHTS?!

CLAIRE. (*Smile*.) Some.

EDNA. Some. Rights and responsibilities. Some.

CLAIRE. (*Seeing* HARRY *in the archway, Off* L.) Hello, there, Harry; c'mon in. Julia's about to fix us all something. What'll you . . .

HARRY. (*Rubbing his hands together; quite at ease*.) I'll do it; don't trouble yourself, Julia. (*Crosses* D. L. *to bar*.)

JULIA. (*Rushes to the bar, her back to it, spreads her arms, protecting it, curiously disturbed and frightened by something*.) NO! Don't you come near it! Don't you take a step!

HARRY. (*Patiently, moving forward a little*.) Now, Julia . . .

JULIA. NO!

EDNA. (*Sitting on sofa, relaxing*.) Let her do it, Harry. She wants to.

JULIA. I DON'T WANT TO!!

HARRY. (*Firm*.) Then I'll do it, Julia.

JULIA. (*Suddenly a little girl; crying*.) Mother!? MOTHER!?

EDNA. (*Shaking her head; not unkindly*.) Honestly.

JULIA. MOTHER!?

CLAIRE. (*The way a nurse speaks to a disturbed patient*.) Julia? Will you let me do it? May I get the drinks?

JULIA. (*Hissed*.) Stay away from it! All of you!

CLAIRE. (*Rising*.) Now, Julia . . .

HARRY. Oh, come on, Julia, now . . .

EDNA. Let her *go*, Harry.

JULIA. MOTHER? FATHER! HELP ME!!

(AGNES *enters*.)

AGNES. (*Pained. At* C. *arch*.) Julia? You're shouting?

JULIA. (*Rushes to* AGNES.) Mother!

AGNES. (*Quite conscious of the others.*) What *is* it, dear?

JULIA. (*Quite beside herself, seeing no sympathy.*) THEY! THEY WANT!

EDNA. (*Crosses* R.) Forget it, Julia.

HARRY. (*A tiny, condescending laugh.*) Yes, for God's sake, forget it.

JULIA. THEY WANT!

AGNES. (*Kindly, but a little patronizing.*) Perhaps you *had* better go upstairs.

JULIA. (*Still semi-hysterical.*) Yes? Where!? What room!?

AGNES. (*Patient.*) Go up to my room, lie down.

JULIA. (*An ugly laugh.*) *Your room!*

EDNA. (*Calm.*) You may lie down in *our* room, if you prefer. (*At* R. *chair.*)

JULIA. (*A trapped woman, surrounded, crossing to* EDNA.) *Your* room! (*To* AGNES.) *Your* room? MINE!! (*Looks from one to another, sees only waiting faces.*) MINE!!

HARRY. (*Makes a move toward the sideboard.*) God.

JULIA. Don't you go near *that!*

AGNES. Julia . . .

JULIA. I *want!*

CLAIRE. (*Sad smile.*) What do you want, Julia?

JULIA. I . . .

HARRY. Jesus.

JULIA. I WANT . . . WHAT IS MINE!! (*Crosses to* AGNES.)

AGNES. (*Seemingly dispassionate; after a pause.*) Well, then, my dear, you will have to decide what that is, will you not.

JULIA. (*A terrified pause; runs from the room.*) Daddy? Daddy?

(*A silence;* HARRY *moves to the sideboard, begins to make himself a drink.*)

AGNES. (*As if very little had happened. Crosses to sofa.*) Why, I do believe that's the first time she's called on her father in . . . since her childhood.

CLAIRE. When she used to skin her knees?

AGNES. (*A little laugh.*) Yes, and she would come home bloody. I *assumed* she was clumsy, but it crossed my mind a time or two . . . that she was religious.

EDNA. (*To* R. *chair.*) Praying on the gravel? A penance?

AGNES. (*Chuckles, but it covers something else.*) Yes. Teddy had just died, I think, and it was an . . . unreal time . . . for a number of us, for me. (*Brief sorrow clearly shown.*) Poor little boy.

EDNA. Yes.

AGNES. It was an unreal time: I thought Tobias was out of love with me—or, rather, was tired of it, when Teddy died, as if that had been the string.

HARRY. Would you like something, Edna?

EDNA. (*Her eyes on* AGNES; *rather dreamy.*) Um-humh.

(HARRY *crosses to bar, makes drink.*)

AGNES. (*Not explaining, and to none of them, really.*) Ah, the things I doubted then: that I was loved—that *I* loved, for that matter!—that Teddy had ever lived at all—my mind, you see. That Julia would be with us long. I think . . . I think I thought Tobias was unfaithful to me then. Was he, Harry?

EDNA. Oh, Agnes.

HARRY. (*Unsubtle.*) Come on, Agnes! Of course not! No!

AGNES. (*Faint amusement.*) Was he, Claire? That hot summer, with Julia's knees all bloody and Teddy dead? Did my husband . . . cheat on me?

CLAIRE. (*Looks at her steadily, toasts her; then:*) Ya got me, Sis.

AGNES. (*An amen.*) And that will have to do.

(HARRY *crosses and hands* EDNA *a drink.*)

EDNA. Poor *Julia.*

AGNES. (*Shrugs.*) Julia is a fool. Will you make me a drink, Harry, since you're being Tobias? A Scotch?

HARRY. Sure thing. Claire?

CLAIRE. Why not. (*Hands* HARRY *glass, and he crosses to bar.*)

AGNES. (*An overly sweet smile.*) Claire could tell us so much if she cared to, could you not, Claire. Claire, who watches from the sidelines, has seen so very much, has seen us all so clearly, have you not, Claire. You were not named for nothing.

CLAIRE. (*A pleasant warning.*) Lay off, Sis.

(HARRY *crosses to her and hands her a drink.*)

AGNES. (*Eyes level on* EDNA *and* HARRY; *precisely and not too nicely.*) What do you *want?*

HARRY. (*After a pause and a look at* EDNA.) I don't know what you mean.

EDNA. (*Seemingly puzzled.*) Yes.

AGNES. (*Eyes narrow.*) What do you *really* . . . *want?*

CLAIRE. You gonna tell her, Harry?

HARRY. (*Steps to bar.*) I, *I* don't know what you mean Claire. Scotch, was it, Agnes?

AGNES. I *said.*

HARRY. (*Less than pleasant.*) Yes, but I don't remember. (*Crosses to bar.*)

EDNA. (*Her eyes narrowing, too.*) Don't talk to Harry like that.

AGNES. (*About to attack, thinks better of it.*) I . . . I'm sorry, Edna. I forgot that you're . . . very frightened people.

EDNA. DON'T YOU MAKE FUN OF US!

AGNES. My dear Edna, I am not mak—

EDNA. YES YOU ARE! YOU'RE MAKING FUN OF US.

AGNES. I assure you, Edna . . .

HARRY. (*Handing* AGNES *a drink; with some disgust.*) Here's your drink. (*Crosses* U. L.)

AGNES. I, I assure you.

CLAIRE. (*Puts on her ACCORDION. Crosses to otto-man.*) I think it's time for a little music, don't you, kids! I yodel a little, too, nowadays, if anybody . . .

AGNES. (*Exasperated.*) We *don't* want music, Claire!

HARRY. (*Horrified and amused.*) You, you *what!?* You *yodel!?*

CLAIRE. (*As if it were the most natural thing in the world.*) Well . . . sure. (*Crosses* U. L. *to* HARRY.)

EDNA. (*Dry.*) Talent will out.

HARRY. (*Continuing disbelief.*) You yodel!

CLAIRE. (*Emphatic; babytalk.*) 'ES!

(TOBIAS *has appeared in the archway.*)

HARRY. She yodels!

CLAIRE. (*Bravura.*) What would ya like, Harry? A chorus of "Take me to the greenhouse, lay me down . . ."?

AGNES. Claire!

TOBIAS. (*Crosses to* U. L. *of sofa.*) I . . . I wonder if, before the concert, one of you would mind telling me why, uh, my daughter is upstairs, in hysterics?

CLAIRE. Envy, baby; she don't sing, or nothin'. (*A chord. Crosses to* R. *of* R. *chair.*)

TOBIAS. (*To the others.*) Well? Will any of you tell me?

AGNES. (*Controlled.*) What, what was she doing, Tobias?

TOBIAS. I told you! She's in hysterics!

AGNES. (*Tight smile.*) That is a condition; I inquired about an action.

EDNA. (*More sincere than before.*) Poor Julia.

HARRY. I don't understand that girl.

TOBIAS. (*Quite miffed.*) An action? Is that what you want? O.K., how about (*Demonstrates this.*) pressed against a corner of the upstairs hall, arms wide, palms back? Eyes darting? Wide? (EDNA *shakes her head. He crosses* D. L. *to* L *of sofa.*) How about tearing into Harry and Edna's room . . . ripping the clothes from the closets, hangers and all on the floor? The same for the bureaus?

AGNES. (*Steady.*) I see.

TOBIAS. More?

AGNES. (*Steady.*) All right.

TOBIAS. Or into your room next? Twisted on your bed, lots of breathing and the great wide eyes? The spread all gathered under her, your big lace pillow in her arms— like a lover—her eyes wide open, no tears now? Though if you come near her the sounds start and you think she'll scream if you touch her? (*Pause.*) How's that?

CLAIRE. (*Pause.*) Pretty good.

AGNES. (*Pause.*) And accurate, I imagine.

TOBIAS. (*Daring her.*) You're damned right! Now, why?

AGNES. (*To* TOBIAS *with a sad smile, ironic.*) Would it seem . . . incomplete to you, my darling, were I to tell you Julia is upset that—Edna and Harry are here, that . . .

HARRY. (*Arms wide, helplessly.*) I was making myself a drink, for God's sake. . . .

EDNA. I asked her to *make* me something. . . .

TOBIAS. Oh, come on!

EDNA. (*Some pleasure. Crosses to bar.*) She rose . . . like a silent film star, ran to the sideboard, defended it, like a princess in the movies, hiding her lover in the closet from the king.

CLAIRE. That sound incomplete to you, Toby?

TOBIAS. (*Stern.*) Somewhat.

AGNES. Julia *has* been through a trying time, Tobias. . . .

HARRY. (*A little apologetic.*) I suppose we did upset her some. . . . (*Crosses to* L. *chair.*)

EDNA. (*Consoling.*) Of course!

TOBIAS. (*To* AGNES; *a kind of wondrous bewilderment.*) Don't you think you should go tend to her?

(*The* OTHERS *all look to* AGNES.)

AGNES. (*Shakes her head; lightly.*) No. She will be down or she will not. She will stop, or she will . . . go on.

TOBIAS. (*Spluttering.*) Well, for God's sake, Agnes . . . !

AGNES. (*An end to it; hard.*) I haven't the time, Tobias. (*Gentler.*) I haven't time for the four-hour talk, the soothing recapitulation. You don't go through it, my love: the history. Nothing is calmed by a pat on the hand, a gentle massage, or slowly, slowly combing the hair, no: the history. Teddy's birth, and how she felt unwanted, tricked; his death, and was she more relieved than lost . . . ? All the schools we sent her to, and did she fail in them through hate . . . or love? And when we come to marriage, dear: each one of them, the fear, the happiness, the sex, the stopping, the infidelities . . .

TOBIAS. (*Nodding; speaks softly.*) All right, Agnes.

AGNES. (*Shakes her head.*) The comings home, the new resolves, departures. Oh, my dear Tobias . . . my life is gone through more than hers. I see myself . . . growing old each time, see my own life passing. No, I haven't time for it now. (*Crosses to* R. *chair.*) At midnight, maybe . . . (*Sad smile.*) when you're all in your beds . . . safely sleeping. Then I will comfort our Julia, and lose myself once more.

CLAIRE. (*To break an uncomfortable silence.*) I tell ya, there are so many martyrdoms here.

EDNA. (*Seeing a hangnail.*) One to a person.

AGNES. (*Dry.*) That is the usual, (*A glance at* CLAIRE.) though I do believe there are some with none, and others who have known Job. The helpless are the cruelest lot of all: they shift their burdens so.

CLAIRE. If you interviewed a camel, he'd admit he loved his load.

EDNA. (*Giving up on the hangnail. Crosses* U. R.) I wish you two would stop having at each other.

HARRY. (*Crosses to bar.*) Hell, yes! Let's have a drink, Tobias?

TOBIAS. (*From deep in thought.*) Hm?

HARRY. What can I make yuh, buddy?

CLAIRE. (*Rather pleased.*) Why, Edna; you've actually spoken your mind.

TOBIAS. (*Confused as to where he is.*) What can *you* make *me?*

EDNA. I do . . . sometimes.

HARRY. Well, sure; I'm here.

EDNA. (*Calm. Crosses to* U. L. *of sofa.*) When an environment is not all that it might be.

TOBIAS. Oh. Yeah; Scotch.

AGNES. (*Strained smile.*) Is that for you to say?

CLAIRE. (*A chord; then crosses* U. R.) *Here* we come!

AGNES. Stop it, Claire, dear. (*To* EDNA.) I said: Is that for you to say?

EDNA. (*To* AGNES; *calm, steady, crossing to* L. *chair.*) We must be helpful when we can, my dear; that is the . . . responsibility, the double demand of friendship . . . is it not?

AGNES. (*Slightly schoolteacherish.*) But, when we are *asked.*

EDNA. (*Shakes her head, smiles gently.*) No. Not only. (*This heard* by ALL.) It seemed to me, to us, that since we were living *here* . . .

(*Silence,* AGNES *and* TOBIAS *look from* EDNA *to* HARRY.)

TOBIAS. Living—
AGNES. Living *here.*
TOBIAS. *Living* here.
CLAIRE. *That's* my cue!

(*A chord, then begins to yodel, to an ump-pah base.* JULIA *appears in the archway, unseen by the others;*

her hair is wild, her face is tear-streaked; she carries TOBIAS' *pistol, but not pointed; awkwardly and facing down. They* ALL *see* JULIA *and the gun simultaneously;* EDNA *gasps but does not panic;* HARRY *retreats a little;* TOBIAS *moves slowly toward* JULIA.)

AGNES. (*Crosses* U. R.) JULIA!

JULIA. (*Solemnly and tearfully.*) Get them out of here, Daddy, getthemoutofheregetthemoutofheregetthemoutofheregetthemoutofheregetthemoutofhere. . . .

TOBIAS. ALL RIGHT.

JULIA. Get them out of here, Daddy!

TOBIAS. (*Moving toward her, slowly, calmly, speaking in a quiet voice.*) All right, Julia, baby; let's have it now.

JULIA. Get them out of here, Daddy. . . .

TOBIAS. (*As before.*) Come on now, Julia.

JULIA. (*Calmly, she hands the gun to* TOBIAS, *nods.*) Get them out of here, Daddy.

AGNES. (*Soft intensity.*) You ought to be horsewhipped, young lady.

TOBIAS. (*Meant for both* JULIA *and* AGNES.) All right, now . . .

JULIA. Do it, Daddy? Or give it back?

(TOBIAS *and* JULIA *cross* D. R. *to* R. *of sofa.*)

AGNES. (*Turns on* JULIA; *withering.*) How dare you come into this room like that! How dare you embarrass me and your father! How dare you frighten Edna and Harry! How dare you come into this room like that!

JULIA. (*To* HARRY *and* EDNA; *venom.*) Are you going?

AGNES. Julia!

TOBIAS. (*Pleading.*) Julia, please. . . .

JULIA. ARE YOU!?

(*Silence, all eyes on* HARRY *and* EDNA.)

EDNA. (*Finally; curiously unconcerned.*) Going? No, we are not going. (*At* L. *chair.*)

HARRY. No.

JULIA. (*To* ALL.) YOU SEE!?

HARRY. Coming down here with a gun like that . . . (*At ottoman.*)

EDNA. (*Becoming* AGNES.) You return to your nest from your latest disaster, dispossessed, and suddenly dispossessing; screaming the house down, clawing at order . . .

JULIA. STOP HER!

EDNA. . . . willful, wicked, wretched girl . . .

JULIA. You are not my . . . you have no rights!

EDNA. *We* have rights here. *We* belong. (*Crosses* U. L. *of sofa.*)

JULIA. (*Crosses to* AGNES.) MOTHER!

AGNES. (*Tentative.*) Julia . . .

EDNA. (*Crosses to* JULIA.) *We* belong here. Do we not?

JULIA. (*Triumphant distaste.*) FOREVER! (*Small silence.*) HAVE YOU COME TO STAY FOREVER?? (*Small silence.*)

EDNA. (*Walks over to her, calmly slaps her.*) If need be. (JULIA *falls on her knees* R. *of sofa.* TOBIAS *comforts her. To* TOBIAS *and* AGNES, *calmly.*) Sorry; a godmother's duty. (*This next calm, almost daring, addressed at, rather than to the* OTHERS.) *If* we come to the point . . . *if* we are at home one evening, and the . . . terror comes . . . descends . . . if all at once we . . . need . . . we come where we are wanted, where we know we are expected, not only where we want; we come where the table has been laid for us in such an event . . . where the bed is turned down . . . and warmed . . . and has been ready should we need it. We are not . . . transients . . . like some.

JULIA. NO!

EDNA. (*To* JULIA.) You must . . . what is the word? . . . coexist, my dear. (*To the* OTHERS.) Must she not? (*Silence; calm. She crosses to* R. *of* R. *chair.*) Must she not. This is what you have meant by friendship . . . is it not?

AGNES. (*Pause; finally, calmly.*) You have come to live with us, then.

EDNA. (*After a pause; calm.*) Why, yes; we have.

AGNES. (*Dead calm; a sigh.*) Well, then. (*Pause. Crosses to* JULIA.) Perhaps it is time for bed, Julia? Come upstairs with me.

JULIA. (*A confused child.*) M-mother?

AGNES. Ah-ah; let me comb your hair, and rub your back. (*Arm over* JULIA'S *shoulder, leads her out. Exiting.*) And we shall soothe . . . and solve . . . and fall to sleep. Tobias? (*She exits with* JULIA. *Silence.*)

EDNA. Well, I think it's time for bed.

TOBIAS. (*Vague, preoccupied.*) Well, yes; yes, of course.

EDNA. (*She and* HARRY *have risen; a small smile.*) We know the way. (*Pauses as she and* HARRY *near the archway.*) Friendship *is* something like a marriage; is it not, Tobias? For better and for worse?

TOBIAS. (*Ibid.*) Of course.

EDNA. (*Something of a demand here.*) We *haven't* come to the wrong place, *have* we?

HARRY. (*Pause; shy.*) Have we, Toby?

TOBIAS. (*Pause; gentle, sad.*) No. (*Sad smile.*) No; of course you haven't.

EDNA. (*Crosses* U. C.) Good night, dear Tobias. Good night, Claire.

CLAIRE. (*A half smile.*) Good night, you two.

HARRY. (*A gentle pat at* TOBIAS *as he passes.*) Good night, old man.

TOBIAS. (*Watches as the two exit.*) Good . . . good night, you two.

(CLAIRE *and* TOBIAS *alone;* TOBIAS *still holds the pistol.*)

CLAIRE. (*After an interval, crossing to arch and turning off a LIGHT switch.*) Full house, Tobias, every bed and every cupboard.

TOBIAS. (*Not moving.*) Good night, Claire.

CLAIRE. (*She turns off another LIGHT switch, then*

crosses to U. L. *sofa, sits on back.*) Are you going to stay up, Tobias? Sort of a nightwatch, guarding? *I've* done it. The breathing, as you stand in the quiet halls, slow and heavy? And the special . . . warmth, and . . . permeation . . . of a house . . . asleep? When the house is sleeping? When the people *are* asleep?

TOBIAS. Good night, Claire.

CLAIRE. (*Rises, crosses; near the archway.*) And the difference? The different breathing and the cold, when every bed is awake . . . all night . . . very still, eyes open, staring into the dark? Do you know that one?

TOBIAS. Good night, Claire.

CLAIRE. (*A little sad.*) Good night, Tobias.

(CLAIRE *exits as:*)

THE CURTAIN FALLS

ACT THREE

Seven-thirty the next morning; same set. TOBIAS *alone, in a chair, wearing pajamas and a robe, slippers. Awake.* AGNES *enters, wearing a dressing gown which could pass for a hostess gown. Her movements are not assertive, and her tone is gentle.*

AGNES. (*Seeing him.* U. C.) Ah; there you are.

TOBIAS. (*Not looking at her, but at his watch; there is very little emotion in his voice.*) Seven-thirty a.m., and all's well . . . I guess.

AGNES. (*Crosses to* L. *chair.*) So odd.

TOBIAS. Hm?

AGNES. There was a stranger in my room last night.

TOBIAS. Who?

AGNES. You.

TOBIAS. Ah.

AGNES. It was nice to have you there.

TOBIAS. (*Slight smile.*) Hm.

AGNES. (*Sits* L. *chair.*) *Le temps perdu.* I've never understood that; *perdu* means lost, not merely . . . past, but it was nice to have you there, though I remember, when it was a constancy, how easily I would fall asleep, pace my breathing to your breathing, and if we were touching! ah, what a splendid cocoon that was. But last night—what a shame, what sadness—you were a stranger, and I stayed awake.

TOBIAS. *I'm* sorry.

AGNES. Were you asleep at all?

TOBIAS. No.

AGNES. I would go half, then wake—your unfamiliar presence, sir. I *could* get used to it again.

TOBIAS. Yes?

AGNES. I think.

68

TOBIAS. You didn't have your talk with Julia—your all-night lulling.

AGNES. No; she wouldn't let me stay. "Look to your own house," is what she said. You stay down long?

TOBIAS. When?

AGNES. After . . . before you came to bed.

TOBIAS. Some. (*Laughs softly, ruefully.*) I almost went into *my* room . . . by habit . . . by mistake, rather, but then I realized that your room is my room because my room is Julia's because Julia's room is . . .

AGNES. . . . Yes. (*Rises and goes to him, strokes his temple.*) And I was awake when you left my room again.

TOBIAS. (*Gentle reproach.*) You could have said.

AGNES. (*Curious at the truth.*) I felt shy.

TOBIAS. (*Pleased surprise.*) Hm!

AGNES. (*Crosses* D. L. *of coffee table.*) Did you go to Claire?

TOBIAS. I never go to Claire.

AGNES. (*Crosses* U. R. *of sofa.*) Did you go to Claire to talk?

TOBIAS. I never go to Claire.

AGNES. (*Crosses to* L. *of sofa, arranges pillows.*) We must always envy someone we should not, be jealous of those who have so much less. You and Claire make so much sense together, talk so well.

TOBIAS. I never go to Claire at night, or talk with her alone—save publicly.

AGNES. (*Small smile.*) In public rooms . . . like this. (*Switches off LAMP on* L. *table.*)

TOBIAS. Yes.

AGNES. Have *never*.

TOBIAS. Please?

AGNES. (*Crosses to* D. L. *of sofa.*) Do we dis*like* happiness? We manufacture such a portion of our own despair . . . such busy folk.

TOBIAS. We are a highly moral land: we assume we have done great wrong. We find the things.

AGNES. (*Sits on sofa.*) I shall start missing you again

—when you move from my room . . . if you do. I had
stopped, I believe.

TOBIAS. (*Grudging little chuckle. Rises, crosses* U. L.)
Oh, you're an honest woman.

AGNES. Well, we need *one* . . . in every house.

TOBIAS. (*Crosses* U. R. *of sofa.*) It's very strange . . .
to be downstairs, in a room where everyone has been,
and is gone . . . very late, after the heat has gone—the
furnace *and* the bodies: the hour or two before the sun
comes up, the furnace starts again. And tonight especially: the cigarettes still in the ash trays—odd, metallic
smell. The odors of a room (*Crosses* D. R. *of sofa.*) don't
mix, late, when there's no one there, and I think the
silence helps it . . . and the lack of bodies. Each . . .
thing stands out in its place.

AGNES. What did you decide?

TOBIAS. And when you *do* come down . . . if you do,
at three, or four, and you've left a light or two—in case
someone should come in late, I suppose, but who is there
left? The inn is full—it's rather . . . Godlike, if I may
presume: to look at it all, reconstruct, with such . . .
de*tach*ment, see your*self*, you, Julia . . . Look at it all
. . . play it out again, *watch.*

AGNES. Judge?

TOBIAS. No; that's being in it. Watch. And if you have
a drink or two . . .

AGNES. (*Mild surprise.*) Did you?

TOBIAS. (*Nods.*) And if you have a drink or two, very
late, in the quiet, tired, the mind . . . lets loose.

AGNES. Yes?

TOBIAS. And you watch it as it reasons, all with a kind
of . . . grateful delight, at the same time sadly, 'cause
you know that when the daylight comes the pressures
will be on, and all the insight won't be worth a damn.

AGNES. What did you decide?

TOBIAS. You can sit and watch. You can have . . . so
clear a picture, see everybody moving through his own
jungle . . . an insight into all the reasons, all the needs.

AGNES. Good. And what did you decide?

TOBIAS. (*No complaint.*) Why is the room so dirty? Can't we have better servants, some help who . . . help?

AGNES. (*Arranges newspapers on coffee table.*) They keep far better hours than we, that's all. They are a comment on our habits, a reminder that we are out of step—that is why we pay them . . . so very, very much. Neither a servant nor a master be. Remember?

TOBIAS. I remember when . . . (*Puts afghan around shoulders.*)

AGNES. (*Picking it right up.*) . . . you were very young and lived at home, and the servants were awake whenever you were: six a.m. for your breakfast when you wanted it, or five in the morning when you came home drunk and seventeen, washing the vomit from the car, and you, telling no one; stealing just enough each month, by arrangement with the stores, to keep them in a decent wage; generations of them; the laundress, blind and always dying, and the cook, who did a better dinner drunk than sober. Those servants? Those days? When you were young, and lived at home?

TOBIAS. (*Memory.*) Hmmm.

AGNES. (*Sweet; sad.*) Well, my darling, you are not young now, and you do not live at home.

TOBIAS. (*Sad question.*) Where do I live?

AGNES. (*An answer of sorts.*) The dark sadness. Yes?

TOBIAS. (*Quiet, rhetorical.*) What are we going to do?

AGNES. What did you decide?

TOBIAS. (*Pause; they smile.*) Nothing.

AGNES. Well, you must. Your house is not in order, sir. It's full to bursting.

TOBIAS. Yes. You've got to help me here.

AGNES. No. I don't *think* so.

TOBIAS. (*Some surprise.*) No?

AGNES. No. I thought a little last night, too: while you were seeing everything so clearly here. I lay in the dark, and I . . . revisited—our life, the years and years. There are many things a woman does: she bears the children—if there *is* that blessing. Blessing? Yes, I suppose, even with the sadness. She runs the house, for what that's worth: makes sure there's food, and not just anything, and decent linen; looks well; assumes whatever duties are demanded—if she is in love, or loves; and plans.

TOBIAS. (*Mumbled; a little embarrassed.*) I know, I know. . . .

AGNES. And plans. Right to the end of it; expects to be alone one day, abandoned by a heart attack or the cancer, *prepares* for that. And prepares earlier, for the children to become *adult* strangers instead of growing ones, for that loss, and for the body chemistry, the end of what the Bible tells us is our usefulness. The reins we hold! It's a team of twenty horses, and we sit there, and we watch the road and check the leather . . . if our . . . man is so disposed. But there are things we do not do.

TOBIAS. (*Slightly edgy challenge.*) Yes?

AGNES. Yes. (*Harder.*) We don't decide the route.

TOBIAS. You're copping out . . . as they say.

AGNES. No, indeed.

TOBIAS. (*Quiet anger.*) *Yes,* you are!

AGNES. (*Quiet warning.*) Don't you yell at me.

TOBIAS. You're copping *out!*

AGNES. (*Quiet, calm, and almost smug.*) We follow. We let our . . . men decide the moral issues.

TOBIAS. (*Quite angry. Crosses above coffee table, throws afghan on* D. L. *chair.*) Never! You've never done that in your life!

AGNES. Always, my darling. Whatever you decide . . . I'll make it work; I'll run it for you so you'll never know there's been a change in anything.

TOBIAS. (*Almost laughing; shaking his head. Crosses* U. L.) No. No.

AGNES. (*To end the discussion.*) So, let me know.

TOBIAS. (*Still almost laughing. Crosses* U. C. *of sofa.*) I *know* I'm tired. I know I've hardly slept at all: I know I've sat down here, and thought . . .

AGNES. And made your decisions.

TOBIAS. (*Crosses* U. C. *to arch.*) But I have not *judged.*
I told you that.

AGNES. (*Almost a stranger.*) Well, when you have . . .
you let me know.

TOBIAS. (*Frustration and anger.*) NO!

AGNES. (*Cool.*) You'll wake the house.

TOBIAS. (*Angry.*) *I'll wake* the house!

AGNES. This is not the time for you to lose control.

TOBIAS. (*Crosses* U. C. *of sofa.*) I'LL LOSE CON-
TROL! I have *sat* here . . . in the cold, in the empty
cold, I have sat here alone, and . . . (*Anger has shifted
to puzzlement, complaint.*) I've looked *at every*thing, *all*
of it. I thought of you, and Julia, and Claire . . .

AGNES. (*Still cool.*) And Edna? And Harry?

TOBIAS. (*Tiny pause; then anger. Crosses to platform.*) Well, of course! What do you think!

AGNES. (*Tiny smile.*) I don't know. I'm listening.

(JULIA *appears in the archway; wears a dressing gown;
subdued, sleepy.*)

JULIA. Good morning. (AGNES *rises, crosses to* D. L.
chair, folds afghan.) I don't suppose there's . . . shall I
make some coffee?

AGNES. (*Chin high.*) Why don't you do that, darling.

TOBIAS. (*A little embarrassed.*) Good morning, Julie.

JULIA. (*Hating it. Crosses* U. L.) I'm sorry about last
night, Daddy.

TOBIAS. Oh, well, now . . .

JULIA. (*Bite to it.*) I mean I'm sorry for having embarrassed you. (*Starts toward the hallway.*)

AGNES. Coffee.

JULIA. (*Pausing at the archway; to* TOBIAS.) Aren't
you sorry for embarrassing me, too? (*Waits a moment,
smiles, exits.*)

AGNES. (*A pause.*) Well, isn't that nice that Julia's
making coffee? No? If the help aren't up, isn't it nice to

have a daughter who can put a pot to boil? (*Crosses to* R. *chair.*)

TOBIAS. (*Under his breath, disgusted.*) "Aren't you sorry for embarrassing me, too." (*Crosses to* U. C.)

AGNES. You have a problem there with Julia.

TOBIAS. (*Crosses* U. C. *of sofa.*) I? I have a problem!

AGNES. Yes. (*Gentle irony.*) But at least you have your women with you—crowded 'round, firm arm, support. *That* must be a comfort to you. *Most* explorers go alone, don't have their families with them—pitching tents, tending the fire, shooing off the . . . the antelopes or the bears or whatever.

TOBIAS. (*On platform. Wanting to talk about it.*) "Aren't you sorry for embarrassing me, too."

AGNES. Are you quoting?

TOBIAS. Yes.

AGNES. Next we'll have my younger sister with us— another porter for the dreadful trip. (*Irony.*) Claire has never missed a chance to participate in watching. She'll be here. We'll have us all.

TOBIAS. And you'll all sit down and watch me carefully; smoke your pipes and stir the cauldron; watch.

AGNES. (*Dreamy; pleased.*) Yes.

TOBIAS. (*Crosses to* AGNES.) You, who make all the decisions, really rule the game . . .

AGNES. (*So patient.*) That is an *illusion* you have.

TOBIAS. You'll all sit here—too early for . . . *anything* on this . . . stupid Sunday—all of you and . . . and *dare* me?—when it's just as much your choice as mine?

AGNES. (*Steps* U. L.) Each time that Julia comes, each clockwork time . . . do you send her back? Do you tell her, "Julia, go home to your husband, try it again"? Do you? No, you let it . . . slip. It's your decision, sir.

TOBIAS. It is not! I . . . (*At sofa.*)

AGNES. . . . and I must live with it, resign myself one marriage more, and wait, and hope that Julia's motherhood will come . . . one day, one marriage. (*Tiny laugh.*) I am almost too old to be a grandmother as I'd hoped . . . too young to be one. Oh, I had wanted that: the *youngest* older woman in the block. *Julia* is almost too old to have a child properly, *will* be if she ever does . . . if she marries again. *You* could have pushed her back . . . if you'd wanted to.

TOBIAS. (*Crosses* D. R. *Bewildered incredulity.*) It's very early yet: that must be it. I've never heard such . . .

AGNES. Or Teddy! No? No stammering here? You'll let this pass?

TOBIAS. (*Quiet embarrassment.*) Please. (*Crosses to* R. *chair.*)

AGNES. (*Remorseless.*) When Teddy died? (*Pause. Crosses* U. R. *of sofa.*) We *could* have had another son; we could have tried. But no . . . those months—or was it a year—?

TOBIAS. No more of this!

AGNES. . . . I think it was a year, when you spilled yourself on my belly, sir? "Please? Please, Tobias?" No, you wouldn't even say it out: I don't want another child, another loss. "Please? Please, Tobias?" And guiding you, *trying* to hold you in?

TOBIAS. (*Tortured.*) Oh, Agnes! Please!

AGNES. (*Turns* L.) "Don't leave me then, like that. Not again, Tobias. Please? I can take care of it: we *won't* have another child, but please don't . . . leave me like that." Such . . . silent . . . sad, disgusted . . . love.

TOBIAS. (*Mumbled, inaudible.*) I didn't want you to have to.

AGNES. Sir? (*Turns in.*)

TOBIAS. (*Numb.*) I didn't want you to have to . . . you know.

AGNES. (*Laughs in spite of herself.*) Oh, that was thoughtful of you! Like a pair of adolescents in a rented room, or in the family car. Doubtless you hated it as much as I.

TOBIAS. (*Softly.*) Yes.

AGNES. But wouldn't let me help you.

TOBIAS. (*Ibid.*) No.

AGNES. (*Irony. A step to* TOBIAS.) Which is why you took to your own sweet room instead.

TOBIAS. (*Ibid.*) Yes.

AGNES. (*A step* R.) The theory being pat: that half a loaf is worse than none. That you are racked with guilt—stupidly!—and *I* must *suffer* for it.

TOBIAS. (*Ibid.*) Yes?

AGNES. (*Quietly; sadly. A step* R.) Well, it was your decision, was it not?

TOBIAS. (*Ibid.*) Yes.

AGNES. And I have made the best of it. Have lived with it. Have I not?

TOBIAS. (*Pause; a plea.*) What are we going to do? About everything?

AGNES. (*Quietly; sadly; cruelly.*) Whatever you like. Naturally.

(*Silence.* CLAIRE *enters, she, too, in a dressing gown.*)

CLAIRE. (*Judges the situation for a moment.*) Morning, kids.

AGNES. (*To* TOBIAS, *in reference to* CLAIRE.) All I can do, my dear, is run it for you . . . and forecast. (*Crosses to sofa* R.)

TOBIAS. (*Glum.*) Good morning, Claire.

AGNES. Julia is in the kitchen making coffee, Claire.

CLAIRE. (*Crosses* U. L.) Which means, I guess, I go watch Julia grind the beans and drip the water, hunh? (*Exiting.*) I tell ya, she's a real pioneer, that girl: coffee pot in one hand, pistol in t'other. (*Exits.*)

AGNES. (*Small smile.*) Claire is a comfort in the early hours . . . I have been told.

TOBIAS. (*A dare.*) Yes?

AGNES. (*Pretending not to notice his tone.*) That is what I have been *told*.

TOBIAS. (*Blurts it out.*) Shall I ask them to leave? (*Crossing to arch.*)

AGNES. (*Tiny pause.*) Who?

TOBIAS. (*Defiant.*) Harry and Edna?

AGNES. (*Tiny laugh.*) Oh. For a moment I thought you meant Julia and Claire.

TOBIAS. (*Glum. Crosses* U. C. *of sofa.*) No. Harry and Edna. Shall I throw them out?

AGNES. (*Restatement of a fact.*) Harry is your very best friend in the whole . . .

TOBIAS. (*Impatient.*) Yes, and Edna is yours. Well?

AGNES. You'll have to live with it either way: do or don't.

TOBIAS. (*Anger rising. Crosses on platform to windows.*) Yes? Well, then, why *don't* I throw Julia and Claire out instead? Or better yet, why don't I throw the whole bunch out?

AGNES. Or get rid of me! That would be easier: rid yourself of the harridan. Then you can run your mission and take out sainthood papers.

TOBIAS. (*Clenched teeth.*) I think you're stating an opinion, a preference.

AGNES. But if you *do* get rid of me . . . you'll no longer have your life the way you want it.

TOBIAS. (*Puzzled. Crosses to edge of platform.*) But that's not my . . . that's not all the choice I've got, is it?

AGNES. (*Crosses to* TOBIAS.) I don't care very much what choice you've got, my darling, but I *am* concerned with what choice you *make.* (JULIA *and* CLAIRE *enter;* JULIA *carries a tray with coffee pot, cups, sugar, cream;* CLAIRE *carries a tray with four glasses of orange juice.*) Ah, here are the helpmeets, what would we do without them.

JULIA. (*Brisk, efficient. Crosses to sofa.*) The coffee is instant, I'm afraid; I couldn't find a bean: Those folk must lock them up before they go to bed. (*Finds no place to put her tray down.*) Come on, Pop; let's clear away a little of the debris, hunh?

TOBIAS. P-Pop?

AGNES. (*Begins clearing coffee table with* TOBIAS.) It's true: we cannot drink our coffee amidst a sea of last night's glasses. Tobias, do be a help.

CLAIRE. (*Cheerful.*) And I didn't have to do a thing; thank God for pre-squeezed orange juice.

JULIA. (*Setting the tray down.*) There; now that's much better, isn't it?

TOBIAS. (*In a fog. Crossing to* D. L. *chair.*) Whatever you say, Julie.

(JULIA *pours, knows what people put in.*)

CLAIRE. Now, I'll play waiter. Sis? (*Crosses to* AGNES *at* U. C. *sofa.*)

AGNES. Thank you, Claire. (*Crosses* D. R. *of sofa.*)

CLAIRE. Little Julie? (*Crosses to* L. *of* JULIA.)

JULIA. Just put it down beside me, Claire. I'm pouring, you can see.

CLAIRE. (*Looks at her a moment, does not, offers a glass to* TOBIAS.) Pop?

TOBIAS. (*Bewildered, apprehensive.*) Thank you, Claire.

CLAIRE. (*Puts tray on table* L. *of sofa.*) Yours is here, daughter, when you've done with playing early-morning hostess.

JULIA. (*Intently pouring; does not rise to the bait.*) Thank you, Claire.

CLAIRE. Now; one for little Claire.

JULIA. (*Still pouring; no expression.*) Why don't you have some vodka in it, Claire? To start the Sunday off?

AGNES. (*Pleased chuckle.*) Julia!

TOBIAS. (*Reproving. Sits* L. *chair.*) Please, Julie!

JULIA. (*Looks up at him; cold.*) Did I say something wrong, Father?

CLAIRE. Vodka? Sunday? Ten to eight? Well, hell, why not! (*Crosses to bar.*)

TOBIAS. (*Quietly.*) You don't *have* to, Claire.

JULIA. (*Dropping sugar in a cup.*) Let her do what she wants.

CLAIRE. (*Pouring vodka into her glass.*) Yes I *do,* Tobias; the rules of the guestbook—be polite. We have our friends and guests for patterns, don't we?—known quantities. The drunks stay drunk; (*Crosses* U. L. *of* TOBIAS.) the Catholics go to Mass, the bounders bound. We can't have changes—throws the balance off.

JULIA. (*Ibid.*) Besides, you like to drink.

CLAIRE. Besides, I like to drink. Just think, Tobias, what would happen if the patterns changed: you wouldn't know where you stood, and the world would be full of strangers; that would never do.

JULIA. (*Not very friendly.*) Bring me my orange juice, will you please?

CLAIRE. (*Getting it for her from tray.*) Oooh, Julia's back for a spell, I think—settling in.

JULIA. (*Handing* TOBIAS *his coffee.*) Father?

TOBIAS. (*Embarrassed.*) Thank you, Julia.

JULIA. Mother?

AGNES. (*Comfortable.*) Thank you, darling.

JULIA. Yours is here, Claire; on the tray.

CLAIRE. (*Considers a moment, looks at* JULIA's *orange juice, still in one of her hands, calmly pours it on the rug.*) Your juice is here, Julia, when you want it.

AGNES. (*Furious.*) CLAIRE!

TOBIAS. (*Mild reproach.*) For God's sake, Claire.

JULIA. (*Looks at the mess on the rug; shrugs.*) Well, why not. Nothing changes.

CLAIRE. (*Crosses to* R. *chair.*) Besides, our friends upstairs don't like the room; they'll want some alterations. (*She sits.*)

TOBIAS. (*Lurches to his feet; stands, legs apart.*) Now! All of you! Sit down! Shut up. I want to talk to you. (*Crosses* U. R.)

JULIA. Did I give you sugar, Mother?

TOBIAS. BE QUIET, JULIA!

AGNES. Shhh, my darling, yes, you did.

TOBIAS. I want to talk to you. (*Silence.*)

CLAIRE. (*Slightly mocking encouragement.*) Well, go *on*, Tobias.

TOBIAS. (*A plea.*) You, too, Claire? Please. (*Silence. The women stir their coffee or look at him, or at the floor. They seem like children about to be lectured, unwilling, and dangerous, but, for the moment, behaved.*) Now. (*Pause.*) Now, something happened here last night, and I don't mean Julia's hysterics with the gun—

JULIA. Look!

TOBIAS. Be quiet, Julia!—though I *do* mean that, in part. I mean . . . (*Deep sigh.*) . . . Harry and Edna . . . coming here . . . (JULIA *snorts.*) Yes? Did you want to say something, Julia? No? I came down here and I sat, all night—hours—and I did something rather rare for this family: I *thought* about something. (*Crosses above sofa to L.*)

AGNES. (*Mild.*) I'm sorry, Tobias, but that's not fair.

TOBIAS. (*Riding over.*) I *thought*. I sat down here and I thought about all of us . . . and everything. Now, Harry and Edna have come to us and . . . asked for help.

JULIA. That is not *true*.

TOBIAS. Be quiet!

JULIA. That is not true! They have not *asked* for anything!

AGNES. . . . please, Julia . . .

JULIA. They have *told!* They have come in here and *ordered!*

CLAIRE. Just like the family.

TOBIAS. Asked! If you're begging and you've got your pride . . .

JULIA. *If* you're begging, then you may not have your pride!

AGNES. (*Quiet contradiction.*) I don't think that's true, Julia.

CLAIRE. Julia wouldn't know. Ask me.

JULIA. (*Adamant.*) Those people have no right!

TOBIAS. No right? All those years? We've known them

since . . . for God's sake, Julia, those people are our *friends!*

JULIA. (*Hard.*) THEN TAKE THEM IN! (*Silence.* TOBIAS *crosses to* D. L. *chair.*) Take these . . . intruders in.

CLAIRE. (*To* JULIA: *hard. Crosses* U. C. *of sofa.*) Look, baby; didn't you get the message on rights last night? Didn't you learn about intrusion, what the score is, who belongs?

JULIA. (*To* TOBIAS.) You bring these people in here, Father, and I'm leaving!

TOBIAS. (*Almost daring her.*) Yes?

JULIA. I don't mean coming and going, Father; I mean as *family!*

TOBIAS. (*Frustration and rage.*) HARRY AND EDNA ARE OUR FRIENDS!!

JULIA. (*Equal.*) THEY ARE INTRUDERS!! (*Silence.*)

CLAIRE. (*To* TOBIAS, *laughing.*) Crisis sure brings out the best in us, don't it, Tobe? The family circle? Julia standing there . . . *asserting,* (JULIA *crosses* U. L. TOBIAS *to* D. L. *chair.*) perpetual brat, and maybe ready to pull a Claire. *And* poor Claire! Not much help there either, is there? And lookit Agnes, talky Agnes, ruler of the roost, and maitre d', *and* licensed wife—silent. All cozy, coffee, thinking of the menu for the week, *planning.* Poor Tobe.

AGNES. (*Calm, assured.*) Thank you, Claire; I was merely waiting—until I'd heard, and thought a little, listened to the rest of you. I thought someone should sit back. Especially me: ruler of the roost, licensed wife, midnight . . . nurse. And I've been thinking about Harry and Edna; about disease.

TOBIAS. (*After a pause.*) About what?

CLAIRE. (*After a swig.*) About disease.

JULIA. (*A step in.*) Oh, for God's sake . . .

AGNES. About disease—or, if you like, the terror.

CLAIRE. (*Chuckles softly.*) Unh, hunh.

JULIA. (*Furious.*) TERROR!?

AGNES. (*Unperturbed. Crosses* U. R. *of sofa.*) Yes: the terror. Or the plague—they're both the same. Edna and Harry have come to us—dear friends, our very best, though there's a judgment to be made about that, I think—have come to us and brought the plague. Now, poor Tobias has sat up all night and wrestled with the moral problem.

TOBIAS. (*Crosses to* L. *table.*) I've not been . . . *wrestling* with some . . . abstract problem! These are *people!* Harry and Edna! These are our friends, God damn it!

AGNES. Yes, but they've brought the plague with them, and that's another matter. Let me tell you something about disease . . . mortal illness; you either are immune to it . . . or you fight it. If you are immune, you wade right in, you treat the patient until he either lives, or dies of it. But if you are *not* immune, you risk infection. Ten centuries ago—and even less—the treatment was quite simple . . . burn them. Burn their bodies, burn their houses, burn their clothes—and move to another town, if you were enlightened. But now, with modern medicine, we merely isolate; we quarantine, we ostracize—if we are not immune ourselves, or unless we are saints. So, your night-long vigil, darling, your reasoning in the cold, pure hours, has been over the patient, and not the illness. (*Crosses to sofa, sits.*) It is not Edna and Harry who have come to us—our friends—it is a disease.

TOBIAS. (*Quiet anguish, mixed with impatience.*) Oh, for God's sake, Agnes! It is our friends! What am I supposed to do? Say: "Look, you can't stay here, you two, you've got trouble. You're friends, and all, but you come in here *clean.*" Well, I can't do that. (*Crosses to sofa.*) No. Agnes, for God's sake, if . . . if that's all Harry and Edna mean to us, then . . . then what about *us?* When we talk to each other . . . what have we meant? Anything? When we touch, when we promise, and say . . . yes, or please . . . with our*selves?* . . . have we meant, yes, but only if . . . if there's any condition, Agnes! Then it's .'. . all been empty.

AGNES. (*Noncommittal*.) Perhaps. But blood binds us. Blood holds us together when we've no more . . . deep affection for ourselves than others. I am *not* asking you to choose between your family and . . . our friends . . .

TOBIAS. *Yes* you are! (*Crosses* D. L.)

AGNES. (*Eyes closed*.) I am merely saying that there is *disease* here! And I ask you: who in this family is immune?

CLAIRE. (*Weary statement of fact*.) I am. I've had it. I'm still alive, I think.

AGNES. Claire is the strongest of us all: the walking wounded often are, the least susceptible; but think about the rest of us. Are we immune to it? The plague, my darling, the terror sitting in the room upstairs? Well, if we are, then . . . on with it! And, if we're not . . . (*Shrugs*.) well, why not be infected, why not die of it? We're bound to die of something . . . soon, or in a while. Or shall we burn them out, rid ourselves of it all . . . and wait for the next invasion. You decide, my darling.

(*Silence*. TOBIAS *walks to the window;* HARRY *and* EDNA *appear in the archway, dressed for the day, but not with coats.*)

EDNA. (*No emotion*.) Good morning.
AGNES. (*Brief pause*.) Ah, you're up.
CLAIRE. Good morning, Edna, Harry.

(JULIA *does not look at them;* TOBIAS *does, but says nothing.*)

EDNA. (*A deep breath, rather a recitation*.) Harry wants to talk to Tobias. I think that they should be alone. Perhaps . . .

AGNES. Of course. (*The three seated* WOMEN *rise, as at a signal, begin to gather the coffee things.*) Why don't we all go in the kitchen, make a proper breakfast.

HARRY. Well, now, no; you don't have to . . .

AGNES. Yes, yes, we want to leave you to your talk. Tobias?

(EDNA *crosses* U. L. AGNES *crosses to* TOBIAS.)

TOBIAS. (*Quiet.*) Uh . . . yes.

AGNES. (*To* TOBIAS; *comfortingly.*) We'll be nearby. (*The* WOMEN *start out,* U. L.) Did you sleep well, Edna? Did you sleep at all? I've never had that bed, but I know that when . . . (*The* WOMEN *have exited.*)

HARRY. (*Watching them go; laughs ruefully.*) Boy, look at 'em go. They got outa *here* quick enough. You'd think there was a . . . (*Trails off, sees* TOBIAS *is ill at ease; says, gently.*) Morning, Tobias.

TOBIAS. (*Grateful.*) Morning, Harry. (*Both* MEN *stay standing.*)

HARRY. (*Rubs his hands together.*) You, ah . . . you know what I'd like to do? Something I've never done in my life, except once, when I was about twenty-four?

TOBIAS. (*Not trying to guess.*) No? What?

HARRY. Have a drink before breakfast? Is, is that all right?

TOBIAS. (*Smiles wanly, moves slowly toward the bar.*) Sure.

HARRY. (*Shy.*) Will you join me? (*Crosses* D. L.)

TOBIAS. (*Very young.*) I guess so, yes. There isn't any ice.

HARRY. Well, just some whiskey, then; neat.

TOBIAS. Brandy?

HARRY. No. oh, God, no.

TOBIAS. (*Pouring.*) Whiskey, then.

HARRY. Yes. Thank you. (*Crosses to above coffee table.*)

TOBIAS. (*Somewhat glum. Crosses to* HARRY, *hands him the drink.*) Well, here's to youth again.

HARRY. Yes. (*Drinks.*) Doesn't taste too bad in the morning, does it?

TOBIAS. No, but I had some . . . before.

HARRY. When?

TOBIAS. (*Crosses to* L. *chair.*) Earlier . . . oh, three, four, while you all were . . . asleep, or whatever you were doing. (*Sits.*)

HARRY. (*Seemingly casual.*) Oh, you were . . . awake, hunh?

TOBIAS. Yes.

HARRY. I slept a *little*. (*Glum laugh.*) God.

TOBIAS. What?

HARRY. You know what I did last night?

TOBIAS. No?

HARRY. I got out of bed and I . . . crawled in with Edna?

TOBIAS. Yes?

HARRY. *She* held me. She let me stay awhile, then I could see she wanted to, and I didn't . . . so I went back. But it was funny.

TOBIAS. (*Nods.*) Yeah.

HARRY. Do you . . . do you, uh, like Edna . . . Tobias?

TOBIAS. (*Embarrassed.*) Well, sure I *like* her, Harry.

HARRY. (*Pause.* TOBIAS *rises, crosses* D. R.) Now, Tobias, about last night, and yesterday, and our coming here, now . . . (HARRY *crosses to bar, puts his drink down.*)

HARRY. I was talking about it to Edna, last night, and I said, "Look, Edna, what do we think we're doing?"

TOBIAS. I sat up all night and I thought about it, Harry, and I talked to Agnes this morning, before you all came down.

HARRY. *I'm* sorry.

TOBIAS. (*Crosses above sofa to* L.) I said, I sat up all night and I thought about it, Harry, and I talked to Agnes, too, before you all came down, and . . . By God, it isn't easy, Harry . . . but we can make it . . . if you want us to . . . *I* can, I mean, I *think* I can. (*Crosses* D. C.)

HARRY. No . . . we're . . . we're going, Tobias. (*Crosses* D. L.)

TOBIAS. I don't know what help . . . I don't know *how* . . .

HARRY. I said: we're *going*.

TOBIAS. Yes, but . . . you're going?

HARRY. (*Nice, shy smile.*) Sure.

TOBIAS. (*Crosses to* HARRY.) But, but you can *try* it here . . . or we can, God, I don't know, Harry. You can't go back there; you've got to . . .

HARRY. Got to what? Sell the house? Buy another? Move to the club?

TOBIAS. You came *here!*

HARRY. (*Sad.*) Do you *want* us here, Tobias?

TOBIAS. You *came* here.

HARRY. Do you *want* us here?

TOBIAS. You *came! Here!*

HARRY. (*Too clearly enunciated.*) Do you want us here? (*Subdued, almost apologetic.*) Edna and I . . . there's . . . so much . . . over the dam, so many . . . disappointments, evasions, I guess, lies maybe . . . so much we remember we wanted, once . . . so little that we've . . . settled for . . . we talk, sometimes, but mostly . . . no. We don't . . . "like." (*He crosses to sofa.*) Oh, sure, we *like* . . . but I've always been a little shy—gruff, you know, and . . . shy. And Edna isn't . . . happy—I suppose that's it. We . . . we like you and . . . and Agnes, and . . . well Claire, and Julia, too, I guess. I mean . . . *I* like you, and you like me, I think, and . . . you're our best friends, but . . . I told Edna upstairs, I said: Edna, what if they'd come to us? And she didn't say anything. And I said: Edna, if they'd come to us like this, and even though we don't have . . . Julia and all of that, I . . . Edna, I wouldn't take them in. (*Brief silence.*) I wouldn't take them in, Edna; they don't . . . they don't have any right. And she said: yes, I know; they wouldn't have the right. (*Brief silence.*) Toby, I wouldn't let *you* stay. (*Shy, embarrassed.*) You

. . . you don't *want* us, do you, Toby? You don't want us here.

TOBIAS. (*This next is an aria. It must have in its performance all the horror and exuberance of a man who has kept his emotions under control too long.* TOBIAS *will be carried to the edge of hysteria, and he will find himself laughing, sometimes, while he cries from sheer release. All in all, it is genuine and bravura at the same time, one prolonging the other. I shall try to notate it somewhat. Softly, and as if the word were unfamiliar.*) Want? (*Same.*) What? Do I what? (*Abrupt laugh; joyous.*) DO I WANT? (*More laughter; also a sob.*) DO I WANT YOU HERE! (*Hardly able to speak from the laughter.*) You come in here, you come in here with your . . . wife, and with your . . . terror! And you ask me if I want you here! (*Great breathing sounds.*) YES! OF COURSE! I WANT YOU HERE! I HAVE BUILT THIS HOUSE! I WANT YOU IN IT! I WANT YOUR PLAGUE! YOU'VE GOT SOME TERROR WITH YOU? BRING IT IN! (*Pause, then, even louder.*) BRING IT IN!! YOU'VE GOT THE ENTREE, BUDDY, YOU DON'T NEED A KEY! YOU'VE GOT THE ENTREE, BUDDY! FORTY YEARS! (*Soft, now; soft and fast, almost a monotone.*) You don't need to ask me, Harry, you don't need to ask a thing; you're our friends, our very best friends in the world, and you don't have to ask. (*A shout.*) WANT? ASK? (*Soft, as before.*) You come for dinner don't you come for cocktails see us at the club on Saturdays and talk and lie and laugh with us and pat old Agnes on the hand and say you don't know what old Toby'd do without her and we've known you all these years and we love each other don't we? (*Shout.*) DON'T WE?! DON'T WE LOVE EACH OTHER? (*Soft again, laughter and tears in it.*) Doesn't friendship grow to that? To love? Doesn't forty years amount to anything? We've cast our lot together, boy, we're friends, we've been through lots of thick or thin together: Which is it, boy? (*Shout.*) WHICH IS

IT, BOY?! THICK?! THIN?! WELL, WHATEVER IT IS, WE'VE BEEN THROUGH IT, BOY! (*Soft.*) And you don't have to ask. I like you, Harry, yes, I really do, I don't like Edna, but that's not half the point, I like you fine; I find my liking you has limits . . . (*Loud.*) BUT THOSE ARE MY LIMITS! NOT YOURS! (*Soft.*) The fact I like you well enough, but not enough . . . that best friend in the world should be something else—more—well, that's my poverty. So, bring your wife, and bring your terror, bring your plague. (*Loud.*) BRING YOUR PLAGUE! (*The four* WOMEN *appear in the archway, coffee cups in hand, stand, watch.*) I DON'T WANT YOU HERE! YOU ASKED?! NO! I DON'T (*Loud.*) BUT BY CHRIST YOU'RE GOING TO STAY HERE! YOU'VE GOT THE RIGHT! THE RIGHT! DO YOU KNOW THE WORD? THE RIGHT! (*Soft.*) You've put nearly forty years in it, baby; so have I, and if it's nothing, I don't give a damn, you've got the right to be here, you've earned it. (*Loud.*) AND BY GOD YOU'RE GOING TO TAKE IT! DO YOU HEAR ME?! YOU BRING YOUR TERROR AND YOU COME IN HERE AND YOU LIVE WITH US! YOU BRING YOUR PLAGUE! YOU STAY WITH US! I DON'T WANT YOU HERE! I DON'T LOVE YOU! BUT BY GOD . . . YOU STAY!! (*Pause.*) STAY! (*Softer.*) Stay! (*Soft, tears.*) Stay. Please? Stay? (*Pause.*) Stay? Please? Stay?

(*A silence in the room. The* WOMEN *come into the room, slowly, stand. The play is quiet and subdued from now until the end.* AGNES *crosses to* U. R. EDNA *crosses to* U. C. JULIA *crosses to* U. L. CLAIRE *crosses* D. L. *to bar.*)

EDNA. (*Calm.*) Harry, will you bring our bags down? Maybe Tobias will help you. Will you ask him?

HARRY. (*Gentle.*) Sure. (*Goes to* TOBIAS, *who is quietly wiping tears from his face, takes him gently by the shoulder.*) Tobias? Will you help me? Get the bags upstairs?

(TOBIAS *nods, the two* MEN *exit. Silence.*)

EDNA. (*Slightly strained, but conversational.*) Poor Harry; he's not a . . . callous man, for all his bluff. (*Relaxing a little, almost a contentment.*) He . . . he came to my bed last night, got in with me, I . . . let him stay, and talk. I let him think I . . . wanted to make love; he . . . it pleases him, I think—to know he would be wanted, if he . . . He said to me . . . He . . . he lay there in the dark with me—this man—and he said to me, very softly, and like a little boy, rather: "Do they love us? Do they love us, Edna?" Oh, I let a silence go by. "Well . . . as much as we love them . . . I should think." (*Pause.*) The hair on his chest is very gray . . . and soft. "Would . . . would we let them stay, Edna?" Almost a whisper. Then still again. (*Kindly.*) Well, I hope he told Tobias something simple, something to help. We mustn't press our luck, must we: test. (*Pause. Slight smile.*) It's sad to come to the end of it, isn't it, nearly the end; so much more of it gone by . . . than left, and still not know—still not have learned . . . the boundaries, what we may not do . . . not ask, for fear of looking in a mirror. We *shouldn't* have come.

AGNES. (*A bit by rote.*) Now, Edna . . .

EDNA. For our own sake; our own . . . lack. It's sad to know you've gone through it all, or most of it, without . . . that the one body you've wrapped your arms around . . . the only skin you've ever known . . . is your own—and that it's dry . . . and not warm. (*Pause. Back to slightly strained conversational tone.*) What will you do, Julia? Will you be seeing Douglas? (*Crosses to sofa and sits.*)

JULIA. (*Looking at her coffee.*) I haven't thought about it; I don't know, I doubt it.

AGNES. Time. (*Pause. They look at her.*) Time happens, I suppose. (*Pause. They still look.*) To people. Everything becomes . . . too late, finally. You know it's going on . . . up on the hill; you can see the dust, and hear the cries, and the steel . . . but you wait; and time happens. When you *do* go, sword, shield . . . finally . . . there's nothing there . . . save rust; bones; and the wind. (*Pause. She crosses and puts down cup on* R. *table.*) I'm sorry about the coffee, Edna. The help must hide the beans, or take them with them when they go to bed.

EDNA. Oooh. Coffee and wine: they're much the same with me—I can't tell good from bad.

CLAIRE. (*Crosses to bar.*) Would anyone . . . besides Claire . . . care to have a drink?

AGNES. (*Muttered.*) Oh, really, Claire.

CLAIRE. Edna?

EDNA. (*Little deprecating laugh.*) Oh, good heavens, thank you, Claire. No. (*Puts down coffee cup on table.*)

CLAIRE. Julia?

JULIA. (*Looks up at her; steadily; slowly.*) All right; thank you. I will. (*Crosses to bar.*)

EDNA. (*As* AGNES *is about to speak; rising.*) I think I hear the men. (*Crosses to sofa.*)

(TOBIAS *and* HARRY *appear in the archway, with bags.* AGNES *crosses* U. R. *of sofa.*)

TOBIAS. We'll just take them to the car, now.

(*They do so, exiting out front door.*)

EDNA. (*Pleasant, but a little strained.*) Thank you, Agnes, you've been . . . well, just thank you. We'll be seeing you.

AGNES. (*Rises, too; some worry on her face.*) Yes; well, don't be strangers.

EDNA. (*Laughs.*) Oh, good Lord, how could we be?

Our lives are . . . the same. (*Pause. Steps* L.) Julia . . .
think a little.

JULIA. (*A trifle defiant, crossing and sitting on ottoman.*) Oh, I will, Edna. I'm fond of marriage.

EDNA. Claire, my darling, *do* be good.

CLAIRE. (*Two drinks in her hands; bravura.*) Well,
I'll try to be quiet. (*Hands one to* JULIA.)

EDNA. I'm going into town on Thursday, Agnes. Would
you like to come? (*A longer pause than necessary,*
CLAIRE *and* JULIA *look at* AGNES.)

AGNES. (*Just a trifle awkward.*) Well . . . no, I don't
think so, Edna; I've . . . I've so much to do.

EDNA. (*Cooler; sad.*) Oh. Well . . . perhaps another
week.

AGNES. Oh, yes; we'll do it.

(*The* MEN *reappear.*)

TOBIAS. (*Somewhat formal, reserved.*) All done.

HARRY. (*Slight sigh.*) All set.

(AGNES *crosses and stands* U. C. *in hallway.*)

AGNES. (*Going to* HARRY.) Harry, my darling; take
good care.

HARRY. Th-thank you, Agnes; you, too, Julia? You
. . . you be good.

JULIA. Goodbye, Harry.

CLAIRE. (*Handing* JULIA *her drink. Crosses to* R.
chair.) 'Bye, Harry; see you round.

HARRY. (*Smiles, a little ruefully.*) Sure thing, Claire.

EDNA. Goodbye, Tobias . . . thank you.

TOBIAS. (*Mumbled.*) Goodbye, Edna. (*Tiny silence.*)

HARRY. Thanks, old man.

TOBIAS. (*Softly; sadly.*) Please? Stay? (*Pause.*)

HARRY. (*Nods.*) See you at the club. Well? Edna?
(*They start out.*)

AGNES. (*After them.*) Drive carefully, now. It's Sunday.

(TOBIAS *crosses to sofa, sits.*)

EDNA'S and HARRY'S VOICES. All right. Goodbye. Thank you.

(*The* FOUR *in the room together.* AGNES *moves to* TOBIAS, *puts her arm around him.*)

AGNES. (*Sigh.*) Well. Here we all are. You all right, my darling?

TOBIAS. (*Clears his throat.*) Sure.

AGNES. (*Still with her arm around him.*) Your daughter has taken to drinking in the morning, I hope you'll notice.

TOBIAS. (*Unconcerned.*) Oh? (*Moves away from her.*) I had one here . . . somewhere, one with Harry. Oh, there it is.

AGNES. (*Crosses to* R. *table.*) Well, I would seem to have *three* early-morning drinkers now. I hope it won't become a club. We'd have to get a license, would we not?

TOBIAS. Just think of it as very late at night.

AGNES. All right, I will. (*Silence.*)

TOBIAS. I tried. (*Pause.*) I was honest. (*Silence.*) Didn't I? (*Pause.*) Wasn't I?

JULIA. (*Pause.*) You were very honest, Father. And you tried.

TOBIAS. Didn't I try, Claire? Wasn't I honest?

CLAIRE. (*Comfort; rue.*) Sure you were. You tried.

TOBIAS. I'm sorry. I apologize.

AGNES. (*To fill a silence. At* U. R. *sofa.*) What I find most astonishing—aside from my belief that I will, one day . . . lose my mind—but when? Never, I begin to think, as the years go by, or that I'll not *know* if it happens, or maybe even *has*—what I find most astonishing, I think, is the wonder of daylight, of the sun. All the centuries, millenniums—all the history—I wonder if that's why we sleep at night, because the darkness still . . . frightens us? They say we sleep to let the demons out—to let the mind go raving mad, our dreams and nightmares all our logic gone awry, the dark side of our reason. And when the daylight comes again . . . comes order with it. (*Sad chuckle.*) Poor Edna and Harry. (*Sigh.*) Well, they're safely gone . . . and we'll all forget . . . quite soon. (*Pause. Then she leans over sofa, touches* TOBIAS.) Come now; we can begin the day.

CURTAIN

PROPERTY PLOT

PRESET—*Off* L.:
  Accordion in case
  Revolver
  Large silver tray with coffee service—4 cups and 4 saucers
  Tray with 4 orange juice glasses
  2 magazines
  1 Double-Crostik—*Saturday Review*
  Suitcase
  Purse
  Coat
  1 piece man's luggage, large
  1 piece lady's luggage, large
  1 lady's overnight case

ACT ONE

PRESET:

  Sofa:
    Large pillow stage R. arm
    Small pillow stage L. arm

  Coffee Table:
    Ash tray
    Cigarette box
    Section *New York Times*

  Table L. *of Sofa:*
    Cup and saucer (demitasse) half-full
    Cigarette lighter
    Ash tray
    Small box of stick matches

  D. L. *Table:*
    Humidor with cigars
    Ash tray

Ottoman:
Daily *New York Times* crossword puzzle

R. *Table:*
Ash tray

Black Table on Platform:
Game

Library Table:
Set of books
Silver tray with demitasse pot, 2 cups and 2 saucers

Sideboard (bar) :
See Prop List following

ACT TWO

PRESET:
2 out-of-town newspapers
Set large piece luggage D. R. of R. chair
Set coat on luggage
Set purse on sofa D. R.
Set ice cubes in bucket
Set large pillow stage L. arm of sofa
Strike glasses from coffee table
Strike demitasse service with tray
Strike newspaper from D. L. floor
Strike newspaper from coffee table
Strike game from R. table
Empty ash trays

Sideboard:
See Prop List following

Scene 1 to Scene 2:
Strike luggage, coat and purse
Strike Martini glasses and brandy snifter from coffee ta-
ble, D. L. table, table L. of sofa
Strike Martini pitcher from sideboard
Set demitasse pot, 4 cups and 4 saucers with silver tray on
coffee table
Set 2 magazines on L. of coffee table

ACT THREE

PRESET:

Set Sunday papers on coffee table

Set magazine section opened on floor L. of coffee table

Set L. back pillow on arm of sofa with square velvet pillow

Set one section newspaper on back of sofa R.

Set afghan on floor and R. arm of sofa

Set small round pillow under afghan

Set Scotch bottle opened on D. L. table

Set highball glass ½ full on D. L. table

Set butt cigar in ash tray on D. L. table

Set five more highball glasses on bar

Set ½ full highball glass on table on platform

Set magazine from coffee table to table L. of sofa

Set cigarette box and ash tray from coffee table to table L. of sofa, on top of magazine

Empty ice cubes from bucket

Place large brandy snifter on section newspaper in C. on coffee table

Empty ice cubes from glasses on set

Set water pitcher D. S. on sideboard

FURNITURE PLOT

Stage Right:
   Small round table
   2 practical chairs

Center Stage:
   1 sofa with 2 small pillows
   2 matching chairs
   Coffee table
   Side table—sofa
   Side table—chair

Down Left:
   Bergere and ottoman
   Side table for above
   Bar

Up Left:
   Table
   Lamp
   Chair

Up Center:
   Round table (center hall)

Center:
   Lamp on table L. of sofa (practical)

PROP LIST

5 ash trays
1 cigar humidor (with hinge top, like a cigar box)
1 complete *New York Times* (with crossword puzzle)
1 table style cigarette lighter
1 table cigarette box, silver
Several boxes wooden matches, small size
1 china demitasse set:
    Coffee pot, 4 cups, 4 saucers
1 silver tray for demitasse set
Liquors for bar:
    Anisette—full bottle
    2 brandy—full bottles
    Vodka—full bottle
    Dry Vermouth—full bottle
    Gin—full bottle
    Scotch—full bottle
    Bourbon—full bottle
2 white bar towels
1 glass Martini pitcher
1 metal Martini stirrer
Glasses:
    10 highball glasses—6 oz.
    5 Martini glasses
    4 liqueur glasses
    4 brandy snifters—medium balloon
    2 brandy snifters—large balloon
1 water pitcher for bar
2 bottles Pepsi-Cola
2 bottles Schweppes Tonic
1 silver ice-bucket, hinged top
Ice cubes each performance
1 fresh lemon each performance
1 bar knife, to cut lemon
1 small wooden tray for cutting
1 large piece lady's luggage—JULIA
1 large piece man's luggage, black—HARRY
1 overnight case   }
1 piece lady's luggage } same color—EDNA
1 *Saturday Review* magazine

3 magazines (*Holiday, Vogue, Bazaar*)
1 lady's coat—JULIA—not costume
1 lady's purse—JULIA—not costume
Cigars for humidor
Accordion
1 pack lady's small cigars
2 other newspapers
1 silver coffee service and tray
    (pot, tray, cream, sugar, sugar tongs)
4 china breakfast coffee cups and saucers
4 silver spoons
4 small orange juice glasses
Tray for orange juice glasses
Orange juice
1 small revolver, not practical
1 complete Sunday *New York Times*
1 light throw rug, like an afghan
1 pack cigarettes

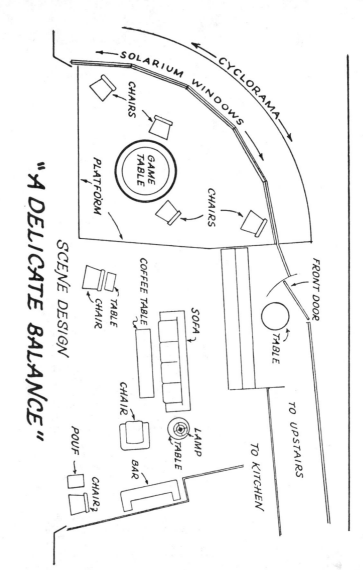

"A DELICATE BALANCE"

SCENE DESIGN

SOLARIUM WINDOWS

CYCLORAMA

CHAIRS

GAME TABLE

PLATFORM

CHAIRS

FRONT DOOR

COFFEE TABLE

TABLE

CHAIR

TABLE

SOFA

TABLE

CHAIR

LAMP

TABLE

POUF

BAR

CHAIR

TO UPSTAIRS

TO KITCHEN